I0781854

HOW TO TRAIN A GERMAN SHEPHERD

Julian Blackwood

Copyright © 2024 Julian Blackwood

All rights reserved. No part of this publication may be reproduced, distributed, or transmitted in any form or by any means, including photocopying, recording, or other electronic or mechanical methods, without the prior written permission of the publisher, except in the case of brief quotations embodied in critical reviews and certain other noncommercial uses permitted by copyright law.

TABLE OF CONTENT

INTRODUCTION

Training a German Shepherd is a crucial aspect of responsible dog ownership, significantly impacting both the dog's well-being and the quality of life of the owner. Proper training ensures the dog develops into a well-behaved, obedient, and mentally stimulated companion. It also helps in establishing a strong bond between the dog and its owner, creating a harmonious living environment. From safety considerations to mental stimulation, the importance of training a German Shepherd cannot be overstated.

One of the primary reasons for training is to provide mental stimulation, which is particularly vital for a breed as intelligent and energetic as the German Shepherd. These dogs are renowned for their intelligence and thrive on mental challenges. Without adequate stimulation, they can quickly become bored, leading to destructive behaviors such as chewing furniture, excessive barking, or digging. Engaging a German Shepherd in training sessions that include learning commands, tricks, and problem-solving tasks helps keep their minds sharp and gives them a sense of purpose. Mental engagement is just as important as physical exercise for maintaining a healthy, happy dog.

Another critical aspect of training is ensuring the safety of the dog and those around it. A well-trained German Shepherd will reliably follow commands, which is essential in potentially dangerous situations. For example, a solid recall command can prevent the dog from running into traffic or approaching aggressive animals. Commands like "leave it" can stop the dog from ingesting harmful substances or objects. By responding promptly to commands, a trained German Shepherd can be protected from harm, and owners can feel more confident about their pet's safety in various environments.

Training also plays a significant role in socialization, which is crucial for German Shepherds. Proper socialization helps these dogs become comfortable and confident in various environments and around different people and animals. Socialization reduces the likelihood of fear-based aggression and helps the dog develop a well-rounded temperament. Training classes and controlled exposure to new experiences teach the dog how to interact appropriately, reducing anxiety and fear in unfamiliar situations. A well-socialized German Shepherd is more likely to be friendly, approachable, and adaptable, making for a more enjoyable and stress-free companionship.

Given the breed's protective instincts, training is particularly important in managing and channeling these instincts appropriately. German Shepherds are naturally inclined to guard their family and territory. Without proper training, this can manifest as overprotectiveness or aggression. Training teaches the dog when it is appropriate to protect and when it should be calm and non-reactive. This balance is crucial for ensuring the dog is a reliable protector without posing a threat to visitors or other pets. Proper training can harness the dog's natural guarding instincts in a controlled and safe manner, making them excellent family protectors.

Training also significantly strengthens the bond between the owner and the dog. The process of teaching and learning commands involves significant interaction and communication, fostering mutual understanding and respect. Through training, the owner learns to read the dog's body language and signals, while the dog learns to trust and rely on the owner's guidance. This bond is foundational for a healthy and fulfilling relationship. Training sessions can be a time for bonding and establishing a strong connection, which is essential for a harmonious living environment.

Training contributes to the overall well-being of the dog. Regular training sessions provide physical exercise, which is crucial for the health of an active breed like the German Shepherd. Exercise helps maintain a healthy weight, strengthens muscles, and promotes cardiovascular health. It also releases pent-up energy, reducing the likelihood of hyperactive or disruptive behavior at home. A well-exercised dog is generally a well-behaved dog, as they are less likely to engage in destructive behaviors out of boredom or excess energy.

Training is not limited to basic obedience; it can include specialized training for various roles such as therapy, service, search and rescue, and protection. German Shepherds are highly versatile and capable of performing a wide range of tasks due to their intelligence and work ethic. Specialized training not only enhances their skills but also provides them with a fulfilling job, which is crucial for their mental and emotional satisfaction. For example, therapy dog training can enable a German Shepherd to provide emotional support and comfort to people in hospitals, nursing homes, and disaster areas. Service dog training equips them to assist individuals with disabilities, performing tasks such as guiding the visually impaired or alerting to medical conditions.

Search and rescue training enables them to find missing persons in various environments, leveraging their keen sense of smell and tracking abilities. Protection training, when done responsibly, can prepare them to guard property or individuals, emphasizing control and obedience to ensure safety. These specialized roles not only highlight the breed's versatility but also provide meaningful and rewarding tasks that utilize their natural abilities and intelligence.

Approaching training with patience, consistency, and positive reinforcement is essential. German Shepherds respond best to training methods that use rewards, praise, and affection to encourage desired behaviors. Harsh methods or punishment can lead to fear and anxiety, undermining the trust between the dog and the owner. Positive reinforcement fosters a positive association with training, making it an enjoyable and rewarding experience for the dog. Training should be a fun and engaging activity that both the dog and the owner look forward to.

Starting training early is beneficial, ideally when the dog is a puppy, but older dogs can also be trained with the right approach and consistency. Early training sets the foundation for future learning and helps instill good habits from the beginning. Puppies are particularly receptive to learning and can quickly pick up new commands and behaviors. However, it is never too late to start training an older dog. With patience and consistency, older dogs can also learn and adapt to new commands and behaviors.

Continuing training throughout the dog's life is important for maintaining and reinforcing good behavior. Ongoing training keeps the dog mentally stimulated and prevents boredom. It also helps reinforce commands and ensures that the dog remains responsive to the owner's guidance. Training should be viewed as a lifelong commitment, not just a one-time effort. Regular training sessions, even if they are short, can provide ongoing mental stimulation and help maintain a strong bond between the dog and the owner.

The importance of training extends beyond the individual dog to the broader community. A well-trained German Shepherd is a good ambassador for the breed, demonstrating their intelligence, versatility, and suitability as companions and working dogs. This helps combat negative stereotypes and promotes responsible ownership. Additionally, well-trained dogs are less likely to be surrendered to shelters due to behavioral issues, contributing to the overall welfare of the canine population. By investing in training, owners can help promote a positive image of the breed and encourage responsible pet ownership.

Training also plays a critical role in reducing the number of dogs that end up in shelters. Behavioral issues are one of the main reasons dogs are surrendered to shelters. Proper training can prevent these issues from developing and help owners manage any problems that arise. A well-trained dog is more likely to be a well-behaved and cherished member of the family, reducing the likelihood of being rehomed or surrendered. Training is an investment in the dog's future and well-being, helping to ensure they remain in a loving and stable home.

Furthermore, training can provide an outlet for a German Shepherd's natural instincts and energy. This breed is known for its high energy levels and drive to work. Providing structured training and tasks can help channel this energy in a positive direction, preventing boredom and frustration. Training can include activities such as agility, obedience competitions, or advanced tricks that challenge the dog both mentally and physically. Engaging in regular training activities can provide a healthy outlet for their energy and help prevent behavioral issues related to pent-up energy.

Training also enhances the dog's ability to participate in various activities and environments. A well-trained German Shepherd can accompany its owner to public places, travel more comfortably, and participate in a wide range of activities. This can significantly enhance the quality of life for both the dog and the owner, allowing them to share more experiences and adventures together. A trained dog is more likely to be welcome in public spaces, making outings and travel more enjoyable and stress-free.

For owners who wish to involve their German Shepherds in specialized work, such as search and rescue, therapy, or service work, training is absolutely essential. These roles require a high level of obedience, focus, and specific skill sets. Training programs for these roles are rigorous and demanding, but they provide the dog with a meaningful and fulfilling job. Specialized training also enhances the dog's skills and allows them to make significant contributions to their community. German Shepherds are often seen in roles that require a high degree of skill and reliability, showcasing their versatility and capability.

The process of training can also be a rewarding and enjoyable experience for the owner. It provides an opportunity to learn about dog behavior, develop new skills, and strengthen the bond with their pet. Training sessions can be a time for fun and interaction, creating positive experiences for both the dog and the owner. The sense of achievement that comes from successfully training a dog can be incredibly fulfilling, providing a sense of accomplishment and pride.

Moreover, training can help address and manage any behavioral issues that arise. German Shepherds, like all dogs, can develop behavioral problems if not properly trained and socialized. Training provides the tools and techniques needed to address issues such as aggression, anxiety, or excessive barking. By addressing these issues early on, owners can prevent them from becoming more serious and difficult to manage. Professional trainers can also provide valuable guidance and support, helping owners navigate any challenges that arise.

Training a German Shepherd is essential for ensuring the dog's mental and physical health, safety, socialization, and ability to fulfill various roles. It strengthens the bond between the dog and the owner, promotes responsible pet ownership, and benefits the broader community. Effective training requires patience, consistency, and positive reinforcement, beginning early and continuing throughout the dog's life. By investing in training, owners can enjoy a well-behaved, obedient, and happy companion, while providing the dog with a fulfilling and enriched life. The importance of training cannot be overstated, as it lays the foundation for a successful and harmonious relationship between the dog and the owner, ensuring a lifetime of mutual trust, respect, and companionship.

Understanding the German Shepherd Breed

The German Shepherd is a breed renowned for its intelligence, loyalty, and versatility. Originating in Germany in the late 19th century, the breed was initially developed for herding and guarding sheep. Today, German Shepherds are known for their roles in various fields, including police work, search and rescue, service dog work, and as loyal family companions. Understanding the unique characteristics and needs of the German Shepherd is essential for providing effective training and care.

German Shepherds are large, strong, and agile dogs, with males typically weighing between 65 and 90 pounds and females weighing between 50 and 70 pounds. They have a distinctive appearance, with a well-muscled body, erect ears, and a bushy tail. Their coat can be medium to long in length, with a dense undercoat and a weather-resistant outer coat. The most common color is black and tan, although they can also be black, sable, or bi-color.

One of the most notable traits of German Shepherds is their intelligence. They are ranked among the top three smartest dog breeds, capable of learning and performing complex tasks with ease. This intelligence makes them highly trainable, but it also means they require a significant amount of mental stimulation. Boredom can lead to problem behaviors, so providing plenty of opportunities for mental and physical exercise is crucial.

German Shepherds are also known for their loyalty and protective instincts. They form strong bonds with their families and are often naturally protective of their home and loved ones. This protective nature can be an asset, but it requires proper management through training to ensure it does not lead to aggression or overprotectiveness. Socialization from a young age is essential to help them develop a balanced temperament and interact appropriately with strangers and other animals.

Their high energy levels and working dog heritage mean that German Shepherds need plenty of exercise. Daily physical activity, such as long walks, running, and playing fetch, is necessary to keep them healthy and happy. They also excel in various dog sports, including agility, obedience, and herding trials. Engaging in these activities not only provides physical exercise but also helps to satisfy their instinctual drives.

German Shepherds are versatile and excel in many roles due to their intelligence, work ethic, and versatility. They are commonly used as police and military dogs, where their skills in tracking, detection, and protection are invaluable. Their keen sense of smell and strong work drive make them excellent search and rescue dogs. Additionally, they serve as service dogs for individuals with disabilities, providing assistance and support in daily tasks.

Despite their many strengths, German Shepherds are prone to certain health issues that potential owners should be aware of. Hip dysplasia is a common concern in the breed, which can lead to arthritis and mobility issues. Regular vet check-ups, a balanced diet, and appropriate exercise can help manage and prevent this condition. Other health concerns include elbow dysplasia, degenerative myelopathy, and bloat. Responsible breeding practices and genetic testing can help reduce the incidence of these issues.

German Shepherds have a strong work ethic and thrive when given a job to do. This can be as simple as learning new tricks, participating in obedience training, or engaging in advanced training for specialized roles. Providing them with a sense of purpose and direction helps to channel their energy and intelligence in positive ways. Structured training sessions and consistent routines are beneficial for their mental and emotional well-being.

The breed's history and development are rooted in its working dog heritage. Max von Stephanitz, a German cavalry officer, is credited with developing the breed in the late 19th century. He aimed to create a versatile working dog that was intelligent, trainable, and capable of performing a variety of tasks. The breed quickly gained popularity for its abilities in herding, guarding, and working alongside humans. Over time, the German Shepherd's role expanded beyond herding to include police work, search and rescue, and service dog roles.

Understanding the German Shepherd's natural instincts and characteristics is crucial for effective training. Their intelligence and eagerness to learn make them highly trainable, but they also require a confident and consistent handler. Positive reinforcement methods, such as treats, praise, and play, are highly effective in training German Shepherds. Harsh training methods can damage the trust between the dog and the handler and lead to fear-based behaviors.

Socialization is a critical aspect of raising a well-rounded German Shepherd. Early exposure to different people, animals, environments, and experiences helps prevent fear and aggression. Puppy socialization classes and controlled interactions with other dogs and people are beneficial. Continued socialization throughout the dog's life is important to maintain their confidence and adaptability.

German Shepherds also require regular grooming to maintain their coat and overall health. Their double coat sheds year-round, with increased shedding during seasonal changes. Regular brushing helps to remove loose fur and prevent matting. Bathing should be done as needed, and attention should be given to their ears, teeth, and nails to prevent infections and maintain hygiene.

In conclusion, the German Shepherd is a remarkable breed known for its intelligence, loyalty, and versatility. Understanding their unique characteristics, including their need for mental and physical stimulation, loyalty, protective instincts, and high energy levels, is essential for providing effective training and care. With proper training, socialization, and care, German Shepherds can excel in various roles and be loyal, loving companions. Their strong work ethic and desire to please make them a breed that thrives on engagement and activity, making them one of the most beloved and respected breeds worldwide.

Setting Training Goals

Setting clear and achievable training goals is essential for successfully training a German Shepherd. These goals provide direction and structure to the training process, ensuring that both the dog and the owner are working towards a common objective. Effective training goals should be specific, measurable, attainable, relevant, and time-bound (SMART). By setting SMART goals, owners can track progress, stay motivated, and ensure that the training is both effective and rewarding.

The first step in setting training goals is to assess the dog's current behavior and skill level. Understanding the dog's strengths and weaknesses allows for the creation of realistic and achievable goals. For instance, if a German Shepherd already knows basic commands like "sit" and "stay," the next goals might focus on more advanced commands or specific behaviors like loose-leash walking or recall. Assessing the dog's behavior also helps identify any problematic behaviors that need to be addressed through training.

Once the dog's current behavior is assessed, the next step is to define specific goals. Specific goals provide clear direction and eliminate ambiguity. For example, instead of setting a vague goal like "improve obedience," a specific goal would be "teach the dog to come when called within five seconds." Specific goals make it easier to plan training sessions and measure progress. They also help to focus efforts on particular areas that need improvement.

Measurable goals are essential for tracking progress and evaluating the effectiveness of the training. Measurable goals have clear criteria for success, such as a specific number of repetitions, duration, or accuracy. For example, a measurable goal might be "the dog will sit on command with 90% accuracy within two weeks." Measurable goals allow owners to objectively assess whether the training is effective and make necessary adjustments to the training plan.

Attainable goals are realistic and achievable within a given timeframe. Setting overly ambitious goals can lead to frustration and disappointment for both the dog and the owner. Attainable goals consider the dog's current skill level, learning pace, and any potential limitations. For instance, expecting a puppy to perform complex tricks within a week is unrealistic, while teaching a basic command like "sit" is attainable with consistent effort. Setting attainable goals ensures steady progress and builds the dog's confidence.

Relevant goals align with the owner's needs and the dog's abilities. Relevant goals consider the dog's natural instincts, personality, and the owner's lifestyle. For example, if the goal is to have a well-behaved companion for family outings, relevant goals might include teaching the dog to walk nicely on a leash, stay calm in public places, and interact politely with strangers. Relevant goals ensure that the training is practical and enhances the dog's role as a companion or working dog.

Time-bound goals have a specific timeframe for completion, providing a sense of urgency and motivation. Time-bound goals create a clear deadline for achieving the desired behavior, which helps maintain focus and momentum. For example, a time-bound goal might be "teach the dog to stay for 30 seconds within one month." Setting deadlines encourages consistent training and allows for timely adjustments to the training plan if progress is slower than expected.

In addition to setting SMART goals, it is important to prioritize training goals based on their importance and urgency. Basic obedience commands, such as "sit," "stay," "come," and "heel," should be prioritized, as they form the foundation for more advanced training. Safety-related commands, such as "leave it" and "recall," should also be high on the priority list to ensure the dog's safety in various situations. Once basic obedience and safety commands are mastered, attention can be turned to more advanced training goals and specific behaviors.

Creating a training plan that outlines the steps to achieve each goal is essential for organized and effective training. The training plan should include a timeline, specific training exercises, and the criteria for success. Breaking down each goal into smaller, manageable steps helps to keep the training sessions focused and ensures steady progress. For example, teaching the recall command might be broken down into steps such as teaching the dog to respond to their name, rewarding them for approaching, and gradually increasing the distance and distractions.

Consistency and patience are key to achieving training goals. Consistent training sessions, using the same commands and cues, help the dog understand what is expected. Patience is important, as learning new behaviors takes time and repetition. Celebrating small successes and being patient with setbacks helps to maintain a positive training experience for both the dog and the owner.

Positive reinforcement, such as treats, praise, and play, is an effective method for achieving training goals. Positive reinforcement encourages desired behaviors by rewarding the dog for performing them. This method creates a positive association with training and motivates the dog to repeat the behavior. It is important to use rewards that are meaningful to the dog, whether it's a favorite treat, toy, or verbal praise. Consistently rewarding desired behaviors helps to reinforce them and achieve training goals.

In conclusion, setting clear and achievable training goals is essential for successfully training a German Shepherd. SMART goals—specific, measurable, attainable, relevant, and time-bound—provide direction, structure, and motivation for the training process. Assessing the dog's current behavior, defining specific and measurable goals, ensuring they are attainable and relevant, and setting deadlines create a roadmap for effective training. Prioritizing goals, creating a training plan, and using positive reinforcement help to achieve desired behaviors and ensure a successful training experience. With patience, consistency, and clear goals, owners can train their German Shepherds to be well-behaved, obedient, and happy companions.

CHAPTER 1

Getting Started

Getting started with training a German Shepherd involves preparation, understanding the principles of effective training, and establishing a positive training environment. The initial stages of training lay the foundation for future learning and success. By setting the stage properly, owners can ensure that the training process is enjoyable, effective, and rewarding for both the dog and themselves.

The first step in getting started with training is to gather the necessary equipment and supplies. Essential items include a sturdy leash, a comfortable collar or harness, and high-value treats for rewards. A clicker can also be useful for clicker training, a method that uses a distinct sound to mark desired behaviors. Additionally, having a designated training area, free from distractions, can help the dog focus and learn more effectively. This area can be indoors or outdoors, depending on the specific training exercises and the dog's preferences.

Understanding the principles of effective training is crucial for success. Positive reinforcement is the most effective method for training German Shepherds. This approach rewards desired behaviors with treats, praise, or play, creating a positive association with the behavior. Positive reinforcement encourages the dog to repeat the behavior and enhances the bond between the dog and the owner. Avoiding punishment and harsh methods is important, as these can lead to fear, anxiety, and a breakdown in trust.

Consistency is a key principle in effective training. Using the same commands, cues, and rewards consistently helps the dog understand what is expected. Inconsistent training can confuse the dog and slow down the learning process. It is important for all family members to use the same commands and training techniques to maintain consistency. This ensures that the dog receives clear and consistent messages about the desired behaviors.

Starting training sessions on a positive note helps set the tone for success. Short, frequent training sessions are more effective than long, infrequent ones, especially for puppies or dogs that are new to training. Each session should begin with a warm-up exercise, such as a simple command the dog already knows, to build confidence and create a positive association with training. Ending each session on a positive note, with a reward or playtime, helps the dog look forward to future training.

Building a strong foundation with basic obedience commands is essential before moving on to more advanced training. Basic commands such as "sit," "stay," "come," and "heel" form the basis for good behavior and control. Teaching these commands involves breaking them down into small, manageable steps and using positive reinforcement to encourage the desired behavior. For example, teaching the "sit" command might involve holding a treat above the dog's head and moving it back, causing the dog to sit naturally, and then rewarding the dog immediately.

Socialization is another important aspect of getting started with training. Exposing the dog to different people, animals, environments, and experiences helps prevent fear and aggression and promotes a well-rounded temperament. Socialization should be done gradually and positively, ensuring that each new experience is enjoyable for the dog. Puppy socialization classes, visits to different places, and controlled interactions with other dogs are effective ways to socialize a German Shepherd.

Crate training is a valuable tool for housebreaking and providing a safe, comfortable space for the dog. The crate should be introduced gradually and associated with positive experiences, such as treats, meals, and toys. Crate training helps with housebreaking by teaching the dog to hold their bladder and bowel until they are let outside. It also provides a safe and secure place for the dog to rest and relax, reducing anxiety and preventing destructive behaviors when unsupervised.

Leash training is essential for safety and control during walks. Teaching the dog to walk nicely on a leash involves using positive reinforcement to encourage walking beside the owner without pulling. Starting with short walks in a low-distraction environment and gradually increasing the duration and difficulty helps the dog learn to focus and walk calmly. Using treats and praise to reward the dog for walking nicely reinforces the desired behavior.

Addressing problem behaviors early is important for successful training. Common issues such as jumping, barking, and chewing can be managed through training and consistency. Identifying the root cause of the behavior and addressing it with appropriate training techniques is essential. For example, jumping can be managed by teaching the dog to sit for attention, while excessive barking can be reduced by providing mental and physical stimulation and teaching the "quiet" command.

Training should be a fun and engaging activity for both the dog and the owner. Incorporating play, toys, and varied exercises keeps the dog interested and motivated. Changing the training environment, adding new challenges, and using different types of rewards can help maintain the dog's enthusiasm for training. Keeping the training sessions positive and enjoyable strengthens the bond between the dog and the owner and promotes a love of learning.

Getting started with training a German Shepherd involves preparation, understanding the principles of effective training, and establishing a positive training environment. Gathering the necessary equipment, using positive reinforcement, maintaining consistency, and starting with basic commands are key steps in the initial stages of training. Socialization, crate training, leash training, and addressing problem behaviors are also important components of getting started. By setting the stage properly and creating a positive and engaging training experience, owners can ensure a successful and rewarding training journey for their German Shepherd.

Choosing the Right German Shepherd

Selecting the right German Shepherd involves careful consideration and a thorough understanding of the breed's characteristics, needs, and your own lifestyle. German Shepherds are highly intelligent, loyal, and versatile dogs, but they also require significant time, training, and commitment. Making an informed decision ensures that both the owner and the dog have a fulfilling and harmonious relationship.

German Shepherds are known for their distinctive appearance, with a well-muscled body, erect ears, and a bushy tail. They are medium to large-sized dogs, with males typically weighing between 65 and 90 pounds and females between 50 and 70 pounds. The most common coat color is black and tan, although other colors such as sable, black, and bi-color also exist. When choosing a German Shepherd, consider the dog's physical traits and how they align with your preferences and lifestyle.

The first step in choosing the right German Shepherd is deciding whether to get a puppy or an adult dog. Puppies are adorable and can be trained from a young age, which allows for shaping their behavior and socialization from the beginning. However, puppies require a significant amount of time, patience, and effort for housebreaking, basic training, and managing their high energy levels. On the other hand, adult German Shepherds may already have some level of training and socialization, but they might come with their own set of challenges, such as unlearning bad habits or adjusting to a new environment. Consider your ability to invest time and effort into training and socializing a puppy versus the potential challenges of integrating an adult dog into your home.

Another crucial consideration is the dog's temperament and energy level. German Shepherds are known for their intelligence, loyalty, and protective nature, but individual temperaments can vary. Some may be more energetic and excitable, while others might be calmer and more laid-back. Assessing your own activity level and lifestyle is essential in finding a dog that matches your energy and daily routine. If you lead an active lifestyle and enjoy outdoor activities, a high-energy German Shepherd might be a perfect fit. Conversely, if you prefer a more relaxed lifestyle, look for a dog with a calmer temperament.

Health is a significant factor when choosing a German Shepherd. The breed is prone to certain genetic health issues, such as hip dysplasia, elbow dysplasia, and degenerative myelopathy. Ensuring that the dog comes from a reputable breeder who performs health screenings and genetic testing can reduce the risk of inheriting these conditions. Reputable breeders will provide health clearances for both the puppy's parents. When adopting from a rescue or shelter, inquire about the dog's health history and any known medical conditions. Regular veterinary check-ups and a healthy diet are essential for maintaining the dog's well-being.

Researching and choosing a reputable breeder or rescue organization is vital for finding a healthy and well-socialized German Shepherd. Reputable breeders prioritize the health, temperament, and socialization of their dogs. They will be knowledgeable about the breed and willing to answer questions about the dog's lineage, health, and upbringing. Visiting the breeder's facility or rescue organization allows for firsthand observation of the living conditions and the behavior of the dogs. A responsible breeder or rescue organization will also ask prospective owners about their lifestyle, experience with dogs, and ability to care for a German Shepherd to ensure a good match.

Considering the purpose for which you want a German Shepherd is also important. The breed is highly versatile and excels in various roles, including companionship, working, and service. If you are looking for a loyal and protective family companion, focus on finding a dog with a balanced temperament that is good with children and other pets. For those interested in participating in dog sports or working roles such as search and rescue, police work, or service dog tasks, look for a dog with high drive, intelligence, and trainability. Understanding the specific traits and abilities required for the intended role helps in selecting the right German Shepherd.

Socialization and early life experiences play a crucial role in shaping a German Shepherd's behavior and temperament. Puppies should be exposed to various people, environments, sounds, and experiences during their critical socialization period, which occurs between three and sixteen weeks of age. A well-socialized puppy is more likely to grow into a confident and well-adjusted adult dog. When choosing a puppy, observe their behavior and interaction with littermates and humans. Look for a puppy that is curious, friendly, and shows no signs of fear or aggression. Similarly, when adopting an adult dog, inquire about their socialization history and observe their behavior in different situations.

Training is an essential aspect of owning a German Shepherd. The breed's intelligence and eagerness to learn make them highly trainable, but they require consistent and positive reinforcement-based training methods. Consider your own experience and ability to provide the necessary training and mental stimulation. Attending puppy classes, obedience training, and working with a professional dog trainer can be beneficial, especially for first-time German Shepherd owners. A well-trained German Shepherd is a joy to live with and can excel in various activities and roles.

Compatibility with other pets and family members is another important consideration. German Shepherds are known for their protective nature, which can sometimes lead to issues with other pets or unfamiliar people. When choosing a German Shepherd, ensure that their temperament and behavior are compatible with existing pets and family members. Introducing the dog to other pets and family members before making a final decision can help assess compatibility. Additionally, consider the dog's background and any previous experiences with other animals and people.

Choosing the right German Shepherd involves careful consideration of various factors, including the dog's age, temperament, health, and purpose. Understanding the breed's characteristics and assessing your own lifestyle and preferences are essential in making an informed decision. Researching reputable breeders or rescue organizations, considering the dog's socialization and early life experiences, and evaluating compatibility with other pets and family members are crucial steps in selecting the right German Shepherd. With thoughtful consideration and preparation, you can find a German Shepherd that will be a loyal, loving, and well-behaved companion for years to come.

Preparing Your Home

A German Shepard in a safe comfortable and stimulating environment

Preparing your home for a German Shepherd involves creating a safe, comfortable, and stimulating environment that meets the needs of this intelligent and active breed. Proper preparation ensures a smooth transition for the dog into their new home and helps establish a positive and structured living environment. This preparation includes arranging living spaces, gathering essential supplies, and making necessary adjustments to accommodate the dog's physical and mental needs.

The first step in preparing your home is designating specific areas for the dog. Establishing a comfortable sleeping area, a designated feeding spot, and a play and exercise area helps create a structured environment for the dog. A comfortable sleeping area can be a crate or a dog bed placed in a quiet and cozy part of the house. Crate training provides a safe space for the dog and aids in housebreaking. The feeding spot should be in a quiet area where the dog can eat without distractions. The play and exercise area should be spacious enough to allow for physical activities and mental stimulation.

Gathering essential supplies is crucial for meeting the dog's needs. Basic supplies include food and water bowls, high-quality dog food, a sturdy leash and collar or harness, a crate, a comfortable bed, and grooming tools. Choose food and water bowls that are durable and easy to clean. High-quality dog food that meets the nutritional requirements of a German Shepherd is essential for their health and well-being. A sturdy leash and collar or harness are necessary for walks and outdoor activities. The crate should be appropriately sized to allow the dog to stand, turn around, and lie down comfortably. Grooming tools, such as a brush, nail clippers, and ear cleaner, are important for maintaining the dog's coat and overall hygiene.

Providing toys and mental stimulation is essential for keeping a German Shepherd engaged and preventing boredom. This breed is highly intelligent and needs regular mental challenges to stay happy and healthy. Toys that promote interactive play, such as puzzle toys, treat-dispensing toys, and chew toys, are excellent for mental stimulation. Regularly rotating toys and introducing new ones keeps the dog interested and engaged. In addition to toys, engaging the dog in training sessions, obedience exercises, and interactive games helps provide mental stimulation and strengthen the bond between the dog and the owner.

Making necessary adjustments to the home environment ensures safety and comfort for the German Shepherd. Childproofing or pet-proofing the home involves securing hazardous items, such as chemicals, electrical cords, and small objects that the dog could swallow. Install baby gates to restrict access to certain areas, such as stairs or rooms with valuable or fragile items. Ensuring that outdoor spaces, such as the backyard, are securely fenced prevents the dog from escaping and keeps them safe during outdoor activities. Regularly checking the fence for any gaps or weaknesses is important for maintaining a secure environment.

Establishing a daily routine helps create a sense of stability and predictability for the dog. German Shepherds thrive on routine and structure, which helps reduce anxiety and promotes good behavior. A daily routine should include regular feeding times, exercise and play sessions, training activities, and rest periods. Consistency in the routine helps the dog understand what to expect and fosters a sense of security. Incorporating training and mental stimulation into the daily routine ensures that the dog's physical and mental needs are met.

Preparing for housebreaking is an important aspect of welcoming a new German Shepherd into your home. Establishing a consistent bathroom schedule, using positive reinforcement, and providing plenty of opportunities for outdoor elimination are key components of successful housebreaking. Taking the dog outside regularly, especially after meals, playtime, and naps, helps establish a routine. Rewarding the dog with treats and praise for eliminating outside reinforces the desired behavior. Being patient and consistent with housebreaking efforts helps the dog learn quickly and reduces accidents indoors.

Socializing the German Shepherd is crucial for their development and behavior. Early socialization helps prevent fear and aggression towards unfamiliar people, animals, and environments. Introducing the dog to various experiences, such as different sounds, sights, and surfaces, helps build their confidence and adaptability. Organizing playdates with other dogs, taking the dog to different places, and enrolling in puppy socialization classes are effective ways to socialize the dog. Positive socialization experiences contribute to the dog's overall well-being and help them become well-adjusted adults.

Regular exercise and physical activity are essential for a German Shepherd's health and happiness. This breed has high energy levels and requires daily exercise to prevent boredom and destructive behaviors.

Incorporating a variety of physical activities, such as walks, runs, fetch, and agility exercises, keeps the dog physically fit and mentally stimulated. Providing a safe and spacious outdoor area for play and exercise is beneficial for meeting the dog's activity needs. Regular exercise not only keeps the dog healthy but also helps burn off excess energy, leading to better behavior indoors.

Creating a positive and structured training environment is important for effective training and behavior management. Using positive reinforcement techniques, such as treats, praise, and play, encourages desired behaviors and strengthens the bond between the dog and the owner. Avoiding punishment and harsh methods is essential, as these can lead to fear, anxiety, and a breakdown in trust. Setting clear boundaries and rules from the beginning helps the dog understand what is expected of them. Consistent training sessions, using the same commands and cues, promote good behavior and learning.

Preparing for potential challenges and seeking professional help when needed is important for a successful transition. German Shepherds, like any breed, may exhibit certain behavioral issues, such as separation anxiety, excessive barking, or chewing. Identifying the root cause of these behaviors and addressing them with appropriate training techniques is crucial. Seeking help from a professional dog trainer or behaviorist can provide valuable guidance and support in managing and resolving behavioral issues. Being proactive and prepared for potential challenges ensures a positive and harmonious living environment for both the dog and the owner.

Preparing your home for a German Shepherd involves creating a safe, comfortable, and stimulating environment that meets the needs of this intelligent and active breed. Designating specific areas, gathering essential supplies, providing toys and mental stimulation, and making necessary adjustments to ensure safety are important steps in the preparation process. Establishing a daily routine, preparing for housebreaking, socializing the dog, providing regular exercise, and creating a positive training environment contribute to a smooth transition and a successful relationship with your German Shepherd. By thoroughly preparing your home and understanding the breed's needs, you can create a welcoming and supportive environment for your new companion.

Essential Supplies and Equipment

Preparing for the arrival of a German Shepherd involves acquiring essential supplies and equipment that cater to their specific needs. This breed is known for its intelligence, loyalty, and high energy levels, requiring items that support their physical health, mental stimulation, and overall well-being. By ensuring you have the necessary supplies and equipment, you can create a comfortable and enriching environment for your German Shepherd.

A sturdy and comfortable crate is essential for providing a safe and secure space for your German Shepherd. Crates serve multiple purposes, including housebreaking, managing behavior, and providing a den-like retreat for the dog. When choosing a crate, ensure it is large enough for the dog to stand up, turn around, and lie down comfortably. Opt for a crate made from durable materials and with proper ventilation. Introduce the crate gradually and associate it with positive experiences, such as meals and treats, to help the dog view it as a safe and comforting space.

High-quality dog food that meets the nutritional requirements of a German Shepherd is essential for their health and well-being. Choose a balanced diet formulated for large-breed dogs, taking into account factors such as age, activity level, and any specific dietary needs or allergies. Look for dog food with high protein content and essential nutrients, such as omega-3 fatty acids for coat health and glucosamine for joint support. Consult with your veterinarian to determine the best diet for your German Shepherd and monitor their weight and condition regularly.

Food and water bowls should be durable, non-toxic, and easy to clean. Stainless steel or ceramic bowls are preferable as they are less likely to harbor bacteria compared to plastic bowls. Place the bowls in a quiet area of your home where the dog can eat and drink without distractions. Provide fresh water at all times and clean the bowls daily to maintain hygiene.

A comfortable and supportive bed is important for your German Shepherd's rest and relaxation. Choose a bed that provides adequate cushioning and support for their joints, especially as they age. Orthopedic beds are beneficial for older dogs or those with joint issues such as hip dysplasia. Consider the size of the bed based on the dog's size and sleeping habits, ensuring they have enough space to stretch out comfortably. Place the bed in a quiet and draft-free area where the dog can rest undisturbed.

Grooming supplies are necessary for maintaining your German Shepherd's coat and overall hygiene. This breed has a double coat that sheds year-round, requiring regular brushing to remove loose hair and prevent matting. A slicker brush and a stainless steel comb are effective tools for detangling and removing debris from the coat. Use a shedding tool or deshedding brush during seasonal shedding periods to minimize loose hair around the home. Nail clippers or a grinder are essential for keeping the dog's nails trimmed and comfortable. Additionally, ear cleaner and cotton balls should be used to clean the dog's ears regularly, preventing infections.

A sturdy leash and collar or harness are necessary for walking, training, and controlling your German Shepherd. Choose a leash made from durable materials, such as nylon or leather, with a comfortable handle for a secure grip. Collars should fit snugly but not too tight around the dog's neck, with enough room to fit two fingers underneath. Harnesses are beneficial for dogs that pull or have neck issues, distributing pressure evenly across the chest and shoulders. Ensure the collar or harness is properly adjusted to prevent escaping or discomfort during walks.

Toys play a crucial role in providing mental stimulation and preventing boredom for your German Shepherd. This breed is intelligent and requires regular mental challenges to stay engaged and happy. Choose a variety of toys that cater to different needs, such as chew toys for teething puppies, interactive toys for mental stimulation, and durable toys for active play. Puzzle toys that dispense treats or require problem-solving skills are excellent for keeping the dog entertained and mentally sharp. Rotate toys regularly to keep them interesting and introduce new toys periodically to prevent boredom.

Identification tags and microchipping are important for ensuring your German Shepherd can be quickly reunited with you if they become lost. Attach an identification tag to the dog's collar with essential information, such as their name, your phone number, and any medical conditions. Consider microchipping your dog as a permanent form of identification, providing a reliable way for shelters and veterinarians to contact you if the dog is found. Keep your contact information updated with the microchip registry to ensure it remains effective in reuniting you with your pet.

Training aids, such as treats and clickers, are useful tools for teaching and reinforcing desired behaviors in your German Shepherd. Positive reinforcement training methods, which reward the dog for good behavior with treats, praise, or play, are effective in shaping their behavior and building a strong bond with you. Choose high-value treats that are appealing to your dog and reserve them exclusively for training sessions to maintain their motivation and focus. Clickers can be used to mark desired behaviors accurately, signaling to the dog that a reward is coming.

A first aid kit tailored for dogs is essential for addressing minor injuries and emergencies at home or on outings. Stock the kit with items such as gauze pads, adhesive tape, antiseptic wipes, tweezers, and a pet-specific first aid guide. Familiarize yourself with basic first aid procedures, including how to administer CPR and manage common injuries, to provide immediate care if needed. Keep the first aid kit in a readily accessible location and replenish any used or expired items promptly.

Environmental enrichment items, such as a variety of surfaces and textures, provide mental and physical stimulation for your German Shepherd. This breed enjoys exploring and interacting with their environment, so provides opportunities for them to engage their senses and satisfy their curiosity. Offer different surfaces to walk on, such as grass, gravel, and sand, to stimulate their paw pads and encourage natural behaviors. Interactive feeders and food puzzles can also be used to make mealtime more engaging, encouraging the dog to work for their food and providing mental stimulation.

Acquiring essential supplies and equipment is essential for preparing your home for a German Shepherd. These items cater to the breed's specific needs for safety, comfort, mental stimulation, and overall well-being. A sturdy crate provides a safe retreat for the dog, while high-quality dog food meets their nutritional requirements. Grooming supplies maintain their coat and hygiene, and a comfortable bed offers a restful sleep. Leashes, collars, or harnesses ensure safe walks, and a variety of toys prevent boredom. Identification tags, microchipping, training aids, and a first aid kit contribute to their safety and well-being. By acquiring these essential supplies and equipment, you can create a welcoming and supportive environment for your German Shepherd, setting the stage for a happy and healthy life together.

CHAPTER 2

Understanding Your German Shepherd

Understanding the German Shepherd breed is crucial for providing appropriate care, training, and companionship. Known for their intelligence, loyalty, and versatility, German Shepherds excel in various roles, from family companions to working dogs. By gaining insight into their history, temperament, and unique characteristics, you can foster a strong bond with your German Shepherd and ensure a fulfilling relationship.

German Shepherds originated in Germany in the late 19th century, developed by Captain Max von Stephanitz with the goal of creating a versatile working dog. They were initially bred for herding and guarding sheep but quickly gained recognition for their intelligence, trainability, and strong work ethic. Today, German Shepherds are valued for their versatility and serve as police dogs, search and rescue dogs, guide dogs for the visually impaired, and loyal family companions.

The breed's appearance is distinctive, characterized by a muscular build, erect ears, and a bushy tail. German Shepherds have a double coat with a dense outer coat and a softer undercoat that provides insulation. The most common coat color is black and tan, although other colors such as sable, all-black, and bi-color are also recognized. Their expression is alert and intelligent, reflecting their keen perception and readiness to work.

Temperamentally, German Shepherds are known for their loyalty, courage, and protective instincts. They form strong bonds with their families and are dedicated to their owners, often displaying affection and loyalty. Their protective nature makes them excellent watchdogs and guardians, as they are vigilant and quick to alert their owners to potential threats. Early socialization and training are essential for managing their protective instincts and ensuring they respond appropriately to different situations and people.

Intelligence is a hallmark trait of the German Shepherd breed, ranking third in Stanley Coren's intelligence list for working and obedience intelligence. They are quick learners and thrive on mental stimulation and challenges. German Shepherds excel in obedience training, agility, and advanced commands, making them highly trainable for various roles and tasks. Their intelligence and problem-solving skills enable them to adapt to new situations and environments quickly.

Energy levels vary among individual German Shepherds, but overall, they are an active and energetic breed that requires regular exercise and mental stimulation. Daily physical activities, such as walks, runs, and play sessions, help burn off excess energy and prevent boredom-related behaviors. Engaging the dog in interactive games, obedience training, and agility exercises not only provides physical exercise but also stimulates their mind and strengthens the bond with their owner.

German Shepherds are known for their versatility and adaptability to various roles and environments. They excel in obedience trials and competitive sports due to their intelligence and eagerness to work closely with their owners. Their versatility extends to roles such as search and rescue dogs, where their keen sense of smell and ability to navigate challenging terrain make them invaluable assets in locating missing persons or disaster victims. In law enforcement, German Shepherds serve as police dogs, assisting in apprehending suspects, detecting drugs or explosives, and conducting search operations.

In addition to their working abilities, German Shepherds are popular as family companions due to their affectionate and loyal nature. They are known for forming strong bonds with their human family members, including children, and often exhibit a gentle and patient demeanor towards them. Proper socialization from a young age helps ensure they interact well with children and other pets in the household, reducing the likelihood of behavioral issues.

Understanding the German Shepherd's need for mental stimulation is crucial for their overall well-being. This breed thrives on challenges that engage their intellect and problem-solving abilities. Providing opportunities for mental exercise through training sessions, interactive toys, and enrichment activities prevents boredom and destructive behaviors. German Shepherds enjoy tasks that involve learning new commands, solving puzzles for treats, and participating in agility courses or scent work.

Health considerations are important when caring for a German Shepherd. Like all breeds, they are susceptible to certain genetic conditions and health issues that potential owners should be aware of. Common health concerns in German Shepherds include hip dysplasia, elbow dysplasia, degenerative myelopathy, and bloat (gastric dilation-volvulus). Responsible breeding practices, regular veterinary check-ups, and a balanced diet contribute to maintaining their health and detecting any potential issues early.

Proper nutrition is essential for supporting the German Shepherd's growth, energy requirements, and overall health. High-quality dog food formulated for large-breed dogs should be selected, taking into account factors such as age, activity level, and any specific dietary needs or allergies. A balanced diet that includes protein for muscle development, fats for energy, and essential vitamins and minerals helps maintain their optimal health and supports their active lifestyle.

Grooming plays a significant role in maintaining the German Shepherd's coat health and overall hygiene. They have a double coat that sheds year-round, with heavier shedding occurring during seasonal changes. Regular brushing with a slicker brush or undercoat rake helps remove loose hair, dirt, and debris from the coat and reduces shedding around the home. Bathing should be done as needed using a mild dog shampoo that preserves the natural oils in their coat and skin. Pay attention to grooming their ears, trimming their nails, and cleaning their teeth regularly to prevent infections and dental issues.

Exercise is essential for the physical and mental well-being of German Shepherds. They require daily exercise to burn off excess energy, prevent obesity, and maintain muscle tone. Engage them in activities such as brisk walks, jogging, hiking, and retrieving games to stimulate their mind and satisfy their natural instincts. German Shepherds enjoy tasks that challenge them both physically and mentally, making them well-suited for activities such as obedience training, agility courses, and scent work.

Training is crucial for shaping the German Shepherd's behavior and teaching them appropriate skills and commands. They are highly intelligent and eager to please, making them responsive to positive reinforcement training methods. Use rewards such as treats, praise, or playtime to reinforce desired behaviors and avoid punishment or harsh corrections, which can undermine their trust and confidence. Consistency, patience, and regular training sessions help establish clear boundaries and expectations for the dog, ensuring they become well-behaved companions.

Socialization from an early age is vital for German Shepherds to develop into well-adjusted and confident dogs. Expose them to various people, animals, environments, and experiences during their critical socialization period, which occurs between three and sixteen weeks of age. Positive interactions with different stimuli help them learn to adapt to new situations calmly and confidently. Encourage positive experiences with strangers, children, other pets, and different environments to prevent fearfulness or aggression as they mature.

Understanding the German Shepherd's vocal tendencies and communication cues helps strengthen the bond between the dog and their owner. They are known for their vocalizations, including barking, whining, and growling, which they use to communicate their needs, alert their owners to potential threats, or express excitement. Pay attention to their body language, facial expressions, and vocalizations to interpret their feelings and respond appropriately. Establishing clear communication through consistent training and positive reinforcement builds trust and enhances the dog's responsiveness to commands.

Providing mental and physical enrichment, maintaining their health through proper nutrition and grooming, engaging in regular exercise, and implementing positive training methods are essential aspects of caring for a

German Shepherd. Understanding their breed-specific characteristics, including their intelligence, loyalty, protective instincts, and versatility, allows owners to meet their needs effectively and foster a strong and rewarding relationship. By investing time, effort, and attention into understanding and caring for their German Shepherd, owners can enjoy a fulfilling companionship with this remarkable breed.

Understanding the German Shepherd breed involves recognizing their history, appearance, temperament, and specific needs for care and training. They are versatile dogs known for their intelligence, loyalty, and working abilities in various roles. Providing appropriate mental stimulation, grooming, nutrition, exercise, and training supports their overall well-being and strengthens the bond between the dog and their owner. By understanding and meeting the needs of the German Shepherd breed, owners can ensure a happy, healthy, and fulfilling life for their canine companion.

Breed Characteristics and Traits

The German Shepherd is a breed renowned for its intelligence, versatility, and robust physical capabilities. These characteristics make them suitable for a variety of roles, ranging from loyal family pets to highly trained working dogs in law enforcement and search and rescue missions.

Physically, German Shepherds are large, muscular dogs with a strong, agile build. They have a distinct appearance characterized by their erect ears, bushy tails, and alert expression. Their double coat consists of a dense outer layer and a softer undercoat, providing insulation and protection in various weather conditions. The coat colors can vary, including black and tan, sable, all-black, and bi-color. Their athletic build and powerful stride are indicative of their working dog heritage, enabling them to perform physically demanding tasks with ease.

One of the most defining traits of the German Shepherd is their intelligence. Ranked among the most intelligent dog breeds, they are quick learners and excel in obedience training, agility, and other canine sports. This intelligence also means they require mental stimulation to prevent boredom and associated behavioral issues. Engaging them in training sessions, puzzle toys, and tasks that challenge their problem-solving abilities is essential for their mental well-being.

German Shepherds possess a strong work ethic and are highly trainable, making them ideal for roles that require discipline and precision. They are often employed as police dogs, search and rescue dogs, and service dogs for individuals with disabilities. Their keen sense of smell and ability to follow commands precisely make them invaluable in these roles. Additionally, their protective nature and loyalty to their handlers ensure they perform their duties with dedication and vigilance.

Despite their working capabilities, German Shepherds are also known for their affectionate and loyal nature towards their families. They form strong bonds with their human companions and are often very protective, making them excellent watchdogs. This protective instinct, however, requires proper socialization to ensure they differentiate between genuine threats and normal social interactions.

Regular exercise is crucial for German Shepherds due to their high energy levels. They thrive in environments where they can engage in physical activities such as running, hiking, and playing fetch. Providing ample exercise not only keeps them physically fit but also helps in managing their energy levels and preventing destructive behaviors.

Health considerations are an important aspect of caring for a German Shepherd. They are prone to certain genetic conditions, such as hip dysplasia and degenerative myelopathy, which can impact their mobility and quality of life. Regular veterinary check-ups, a balanced diet, and maintaining a healthy weight are essential for managing these health risks. Responsible breeding practices also play a crucial role in reducing the prevalence of genetic disorders within the breed.

Behavior and Temperament

Understanding the behavior and temperament of a German Shepherd is essential for providing effective training and care. Known for their loyalty, courage, and protective instincts, German Shepherds display a range of behaviors that reflect their deep bond with their owners and their innate working abilities.

German Shepherds are naturally protective and alert, traits that make them excellent guard dogs. They are vigilant and quick to respond to unfamiliar stimuli, often barking to alert their owners of potential threats. This protective nature, while beneficial for security, necessitates proper training and socialization to prevent overprotectiveness or aggression. Introducing the dog to various people, environments, and situations from a young age helps them develop confidence and appropriate social behaviors.

Loyalty is a hallmark of the German Shepherd's temperament. They form strong attachments to their families and are often very affectionate and attentive to their owners. This loyalty extends to their willingness to protect their loved ones, sometimes placing themselves in harm's way to ensure their family's safety. Their affectionate nature makes them excellent companions, and they often seek close physical contact with their owners.

German Shepherds are also known for their high energy levels and playfulness. They enjoy engaging in activities that challenge both their physical and mental capabilities. Providing regular exercise and playtime is essential for their well-being, helping to channel their energy in positive ways. Without sufficient physical activity, German Shepherds can become bored and develop behavioral issues such as excessive barking, chewing, or digging.

Socialization is key to ensuring that German Shepherds develop into well-adjusted adults. Early and consistent exposure to different environments, people, and animals helps them become confident and adaptable. Socialization also plays a crucial role in managing their natural protective instincts, teaching them to distinguish between normal social interactions and genuine threats. Positive reinforcement techniques, such as treats and praise, are effective in encouraging desired behaviors and building a strong bond with the dog.

Training a German Shepherd requires consistency, patience, and positive reinforcement. Their intelligence and eagerness to please make them highly trainable, but they can also be strong-willed. Establishing clear rules and boundaries from the beginning helps the dog understand what is expected of them. Training sessions should be kept short and engaging, using rewards such as treats, praise, or playtime to reinforce good behavior. Avoiding harsh corrections or punishment is essential, as these can undermine the dog's trust and confidence.

German Shepherds are sensitive to their owners' emotions and can often sense their moods. This sensitivity makes them excellent companions for individuals who require emotional support, as they are intuitive and responsive to their owners' needs. However, it also means that they can be affected by stress or tension in their environment, emphasizing the importance of providing a calm and stable home.

While German Shepherds are generally good with children, it is important to supervise interactions, especially with younger kids. Teaching children how to interact respectfully and gently with the dog helps prevent accidental harm and ensures a positive relationship between the dog and the children. Similarly, introducing the dog to other pets in the household gradually and under controlled conditions helps them develop harmonious relationships.

Communication and Body Language

Effective communication with a German Shepherd involves understanding their body language and vocal cues. These dogs are highly expressive and use a range of signals to convey their emotions, intentions, and needs. Interpreting these signals accurately helps strengthen the bond between the dog and their owner and ensures appropriate responses to their behavior.

German Shepherds use their body posture, facial expressions, and tail movements to communicate. An alert and confident dog will stand tall with ears perked forward, eyes focused, and tail held high. This posture indicates attentiveness and readiness to engage. Conversely, a dog that feels threatened or submissive may lower their body, tuck their tail between their legs, and avoid direct eye contact. Understanding these postures helps owners gauge their dog's comfort level in different situations.

Ears play a significant role in a German Shepherd's communication. Erect and forward-facing ears indicate alertness and curiosity, while ears held back against the head can signal fear, anxiety, or submission. Observing the position and movement of the ears provides valuable insights into the dog's emotional state.

Tail movements also convey a range of emotions. A wagging tail usually signifies happiness and excitement, but the speed and height of the wag can provide additional context. A slow, gentle wag often indicates a relaxed and content dog, while a rapid, high wagging tail can signify heightened excitement or agitation. A tail held low or tucked between the legs indicates fear or submission, while a stiff, upright tail can signal alertness or aggression.

Facial expressions are another key aspect of canine communication. A relaxed dog will have soft eyes, a slightly open mouth, and a calm expression. Dilated pupils, a tense mouth, and visible whites of the eyes can indicate stress or fear. Observing these subtle cues helps owners respond appropriately to their dog's needs and emotions.

Vocalizations are an important part of how German Shepherds communicate. They use a variety of sounds, including barking, whining, growling, and howling, to express different messages. Barking can serve multiple purposes, such as alerting to potential threats, seeking attention, or expressing excitement. Understanding the context and pitch of the bark helps determine its meaning. For example, a high-pitched, rapid bark may indicate excitement or playfulness, while a deep, slow bark can signal a warning or alert.

Whining is often a sign of distress, anxiety, or a request for attention. It can occur when a dog is left alone, feels anxious about a situation, or desires something such as food or a toy. Addressing the underlying cause of the whining, whether it's separation anxiety or a specific need, helps alleviate the behavior.

Growling is a clear indicator of discomfort, fear, or aggression. It is important to take growling seriously and identify the cause, whether it's a perceived threat, territorial behavior, or pain. Addressing the underlying issue and ensuring the dog feels safe and secure is essential in preventing escalation.

Howling is less common but can occur in response to certain triggers such as sirens, other dogs howling, or loneliness. Understanding the specific context and addressing any underlying issues, such as separation anxiety, helps manage howling behavior.

In addition to vocalizations, German Shepherds use physical contact to communicate. Leaning against their owner, nuzzling, or placing a paw on a person's lap are gestures of affection and a desire for attention. Conversely, avoiding physical contact, cowering, or moving away can indicate fear, discomfort, or a need for space. Respecting these signals and responding with appropriate actions, such as providing comfort or space, helps build trust and a positive relationship.

Training and positive reinforcement play a crucial role in enhancing communication with a German Shepherd. Teaching them commands and cues, such as "sit," "stay," and "come," provides a structured way for them to understand and respond to their owner's expectations.

Using consistent signals and rewards reinforces desired behaviors and strengthens the dog's understanding of their role and actions.

Socialization is another key factor in improving communication. Exposing German Shepherds to various people, animals, and environments helps them develop confidence and adaptability. Positive experiences during socialization help them learn appropriate social behaviors and responses, reducing the likelihood of fear-based reactions or aggression.

Understanding the German Shepherd's breed characteristics, behavior, and communication methods is essential for effective training and a strong bond between the dog and their owner. Recognizing their intelligence, loyalty, and protective instincts allows owners to meet their needs and provide appropriate care. By interpreting their body language, vocalizations, and expressions, owners can respond to their dog's needs and emotions, ensuring a harmonious and fulfilling relationship. Through consistent training, positive reinforcement, and proper socialization, German Shepherds can thrive as loyal companions and capable working dogs, enriching the lives of their owners and fulfilling their roles with dedication and enthusiasm.

CHAPTER 3

Basic Training Principles

Positive Reinforcement Techniques

Training dogs using positive reinforcement techniques is widely regarded as one of the most effective and humane methods available. This approach revolves around rewarding desired behaviors to encourage their repetition, making the training process both enjoyable and constructive for the dog. Understanding and implementing positive reinforcement techniques can significantly enhance the bond between the dog and its owner, leading to a well-behaved and happy companion.

Positive reinforcement is grounded in the principles of operant conditioning, a theory developed by B.F. Skinner. This theory posits that behaviors followed by pleasant consequences are more likely to be repeated, while behaviors followed by unpleasant consequences are less likely to occur. In the context of dog training, this means that rewarding a dog for good behavior increases the likelihood that the behavior will be repeated.

A trainer is holding a small treat and giving a clear hand signal for the dog to sit, with a treat in her hand

One of the primary tools of positive reinforcement is the use of treats. Treats are a powerful motivator for dogs, and their immediate and consistent delivery following a desired behavior helps the dog make the connection between the behavior and the reward. For example, when teaching a dog to sit, the owner holds a treat above the dog's head and moves it backward. As the dog follows the treat, its bottom naturally lowers to the ground. The moment the dog sits, the owner rewards it with treats and verbal praise such as "Good sit!" This immediate reward helps the dog understand that sitting leads to positive outcomes.

In addition to treats, verbal praise and physical affection are also effective forms of positive reinforcement. Dogs are social animals and thrive on attention and approval from their owners. A simple "Good boy!" or "Good girl!" accompanied by a pat or scratch behind the ears can be very rewarding for a dog. Some dogs might even prefer playtime or a favorite toy over treats as a reward. The key is to find what motivates the individual dog and use that as a reward for good behavior.

Consistency is crucial when using positive reinforcement techniques. Dogs learn best when the rules and rewards are clear and consistent. This means always rewarding the desired behavior and ensuring that all family members use the same commands and rewards. If one person rewards the dog for sitting while another person ignores the behavior, the dog may become confused and less likely to repeat the behavior. Consistent training helps the dog understand exactly what is expected and what will be rewarded.

Timing is another critical aspect of positive reinforcement. For the reward to be effective, it must be delivered immediately after the desired behavior. Dogs live in the moment, and a delay of even a few seconds can make it difficult for the dog to connect the behavior with the reward. For example, if a dog sits on command but the treat is given several seconds later, the dog may not understand that the treat is for sitting. Immediate reinforcement ensures a clear association between the behavior and the reward.

Training sessions should be kept short and frequent to maintain the dog's attention and enthusiasm. A typical session might last 5-10 minutes and include several repetitions of the desired behavior. This approach prevents the dog from becoming bored or frustrated and helps reinforce the behavior through repetition. If the dog starts to lose interest or becomes distracted, it is better to end the session on a positive note and try again later.

Positive reinforcement can be used to teach a wide variety of behaviors, from basic commands like sit, stay, and come, to more complex tricks and behaviors. For example, teaching a dog to come when called involves rewarding the dog every time it responds to the command. Starting in a low-distraction environment, the owner calls the dog's name followed by the command "come." When the dog comes to the owner, it is rewarded with a treat and praise. Gradually increasing the level of distraction and distance helps the dog learn to come when called in various situations.

Another important aspect of positive reinforcement is using it to address and modify undesirable behaviors. For example, if a dog tends to jump on people when greeting them, positive reinforcement can be used to teach an alternative behavior. The owner can train the dog to sit when greeting people by rewarding the dog for sitting calmly and ignoring the jumping behavior. Over time, the dog learns that sitting leads to attention and rewards, while jumping does not.

Patience is a key virtue in positive reinforcement training. Dogs, like humans, need time to learn and master new behaviors. It is important to be patient and persistent, especially when the dog is learning a new behavior or if the training process is challenging. Every dog learns at its own pace, and some behaviors may take longer to learn than others. Breaking the training into small, manageable steps and celebrating small successes can help maintain motivation and progress.

In addition to patience, maintaining a calm and positive demeanor during training is essential. Dogs are highly attuned to their owner's emotions and can become stressed or anxious if they sense frustration or anger. Keeping training sessions upbeat and enjoyable helps the dog remain relaxed and engaged. If a particular training session is not going well, it is better to end it on a positive note with a command the dog knows well rather than pushing through frustration.

Positive reinforcement also extends to socialization, which is a critical component of a dog's development. Socializing a dog involves exposing it to a variety of people, animals, environments, and experiences in a positive and controlled manner. This helps the dog become well-adjusted and confident in different situations. Rewarding the dog for calm and appropriate behavior during socialization experiences reinforces these positive behaviors and helps prevent fear and aggression.

When training a dog, it is important to use clear and simple commands. Dogs do not understand complex language, so commands should be short and distinct, such as "sit," "stay," "come," and "down." Using consistent commands and hand signals helps the dog understand what is being asked. For example, when teaching the "down" command, the owner can hold a treat in front of the dog's nose and slowly lower it to the ground. As the dog follows the treat and lies down, it is immediately rewarded with the treat and praise.

Repeating this process with the same command and hand signal helps reinforce the behavior.

Leash training is another area where positive reinforcement can be highly effective. Many dogs pull on the leash during walks, which can be frustrating for both the dog and the owner. Positive reinforcement can teach the dog to walk calmly on a loose leash. The owner rewards the dog for walking beside them without pulling, using treats and praise. If the dog starts to pull, the owner stops walking and waits for the dog to return to their side before continuing. This teaches the dog that pulling leads to a stop, while walking calmly leads to progress and rewards.

Crate training is another common training goal where positive reinforcement can be very helpful. A crate provides a safe and secure space for the dog and can be useful for house training and preventing destructive behaviors when unsupervised. The goal is to make the crate a positive place for the dog. This can be done by gradually introducing the dog to the crate with treats and praise. Initially, the owner can place treats and toys inside the crate and encourage the dog to explore it. Once the dog is comfortable, the owner can begin closing the door for short periods, gradually increasing the duration as the dog becomes more comfortable. The dog is always rewarded for entering and remaining calm in the crate, making it a positive and welcoming space.

House training is another critical aspect of dog training where positive reinforcement plays a key role. Teaching a dog to eliminate in an appropriate area involves taking the dog to the designated spot regularly and rewarding it for eliminating there. Consistency is crucial, as well as watching for signs that the dog needs to go outside, such as sniffing or circling. When the dog eliminates in the appropriate spot, it is immediately rewarded with treats and praise. Over time, the dog learns that eliminating outside leads to positive outcomes.

Impulse control is another important behavior that can be taught using positive reinforcement. Teaching a dog to wait patiently or leave an object alone requires self-control and can be very beneficial in everyday situations. For example, the "leave it" command teaches the dog to ignore a tempting object. The owner shows the dog a treat, says "leave it," and then waits for the dog to look away or move back. The dog is then rewarded with a different treat. This teaches the dog that leaving the object alone leads to a reward, reinforcing self-control.

Understanding a dog's body language is crucial for effective training. Dogs communicate their feelings through their body posture, facial expressions, and vocalizations. Being attuned to these signals helps the owner understand when the dog is stressed, anxious, or comfortable. For example, a dog with a relaxed body and wagging tail is likely happy and receptive, while a dog with a stiff body and ears back may be fearful or anxious. Recognizing these cues allows the owner to adjust the training approach as needed to ensure the dog remains comfortable and engaged.

Grooming and handling are also important aspects of training that can benefit from positive reinforcement. Many dogs are uncomfortable with being groomed or handled, which can lead to stress and resistance. Using positive reinforcement to desensitize the dog to grooming activities, such as brushing or nail trimming, helps the dog become more comfortable with these procedures. This can be done by rewarding the dog for calm behavior during grooming and gradually increasing the duration and intensity of the grooming sessions.

Incorporating enrichment activities into the training routine is essential for keeping the dog mentally and physically stimulated. Puzzle toys, agility courses, and scent work are examples of activities that provide mental stimulation and challenge the dog in new ways. These activities can be rewarding and enjoyable for the dog, and incorporating positive reinforcement helps reinforce the desired behaviors. For example, rewarding the dog for successfully navigating an agility course or solving a puzzle toy encourages the dog to engage with these activities and develop problem-solving skills.

Behavioral issue management is another area where positive reinforcement can be very effective. Many dogs develop undesirable behaviors, such as excessive barking, chewing, or digging, due to boredom, anxiety, or lack of training. Identifying the underlying cause of the behavior and using positive reinforcement to teach alternative behaviors can help address these issues. For example, if a dog is barking excessively out of boredom, providing mental stimulation through puzzle toys or training sessions can help reduce the barking. Rewarding the dog for quiet behavior and redirecting its energy to positive activities helps modify the undesirable behavior.

In summary, positive reinforcement techniques are a humane and effective way to train dogs. By rewarding desired behaviors, maintaining consistency, being patient, and setting clear boundaries, owners can help their dogs learn and develop good behaviors. Positive reinforcement not only helps in teaching basic commands but also in addressing behavioral issues and enhancing the overall relationship between the dog and its owner. The key to successful training lies in understanding what motivates the dog, using immediate and consistent rewards, and maintaining a calm and positive demeanor throughout the training process. Through these techniques, training becomes a rewarding and enjoyable experience for both the dog and the owner, leading to a well-behaved and happy canine companion.

Consistency and Patience

Consistency and patience form the cornerstone of effective dog training, influencing not only the dog's behavior but also the quality of the relationship between the dog and its owner. These principles ensure that training is effective, humane, and enduring, fostering a well-behaved and happy companion.

Consistency in dog training involves the uniform application of commands, rewards, and corrections. This uniformity helps dogs understand expectations and reinforces desired behaviors. When commands and rewards are applied consistently, dogs can more easily associate specific actions with outcomes, simplifying the learning process. For instance, if training a dog to sit, the command "sit" should always be given in the same tone of voice and with the same hand signal. If the dog sits, it should be immediately rewarded with a treat or praise. Inconsistent commands or delayed rewards can confuse the dog, hindering its learning process.

The timing of training sessions is also crucial for consistency. Regular, short training sessions are more effective than sporadic, lengthy ones. For example, ten-minute sessions conducted two to three times a day help keep the dog engaged and focused. Dogs, especially young ones, have short attention spans, and frequent, brief sessions maintain their interest and enthusiasm for learning. This regularity helps establish a routine, making training a predictable and comfortable part of the dog's daily life.

Consistency extends to the location of training sessions. Initially, training should take place in a quiet, distraction-free environment where the dog can fully concentrate. As the dog becomes more proficient in responding to commands, training sessions can gradually be moved to more challenging environments with more distractions. This progression helps the dog learn to obey commands in various situations, reinforcing the behavior regardless of the setting.

Moreover, all family members must follow the same training protocols to ensure consistency. If one person allows the dog on the couch while another scolds it for the same behavior, the dog receives mixed signals, leading to confusion. Consistency in commands, signals, and rules ensures the dog receives a clear message from everyone in the household.

Patience, on the other hand, involves understanding that learning is a gradual process and that mistakes are part of that process. Dogs, like humans, need time to learn and master new skills. Patience means staying calm and composed, even when progress seems slow or when the dog does not immediately understand what is being asked.

Training a dog requires maintaining a calm and positive attitude. Dogs are sensitive to their owner's emotions and can easily pick up on frustration or impatience. If an owner becomes frustrated, the dog may become anxious or stressed, which can hinder the learning process. Keeping training sessions upbeat and enjoyable helps the dog remain relaxed and engaged. If a particular session is not going well, it is better to end it on a positive note with a command the dog knows well rather than pushing through frustration.

Breaking down training tasks into smaller, more manageable steps is a practical way to exercise patience. For example, when teaching a dog to lie down, the owner might first reward the dog for lowering its head, then for bending its front legs, and finally for lying down completely. Each small step is rewarded and reinforced, gradually leading to the final desired behavior. This incremental approach helps prevent the dog from becoming overwhelmed and makes the training process more achievable and enjoyable.

Celebrating small successes is another important aspect of patience. Every small step toward the desired behavior is a victory and should be acknowledged with praise and rewards. This positive reinforcement not only motivates the dog but also helps build its confidence. Every dog learns at its own pace, and what works for one dog might not work for another. Being patient and adaptable to the individual needs and learning style of the dog is crucial for successful training.

Consistency and patience are not only important for training specific commands but also for addressing behavioral issues. For example, if a dog exhibits undesirable behavior such as excessive barking, the owner must consistently apply the chosen method of correction every time the behavior occurs. This might involve ignoring the barking and rewarding the dog when it stops or using a command like "quiet" followed by a reward when the dog complies. Consistency in addressing the behavior helps the dog understand what is expected and what is not acceptable.

Similarly, patience is required when addressing behavioral issues. Some behaviors may take time to change, especially if they have been reinforced inadvertently over a long period. It is important to remain patient and persistent, knowing that progress may be slow but that consistent effort will eventually lead to improvement.

Consistency and patience are also vital when socializing a dog. Socialization involves exposing the dog to a variety of people, animals, environments, and experiences in a positive and controlled manner. Consistently rewarding the dog for calm and appropriate behavior during these experiences helps reinforce positive associations. Patience is required to gradually introduce the dog to new experiences and to allow it time to adjust and become comfortable.

When socializing a dog, it is important to start with less challenging situations and gradually increase the level of difficulty. For example, the owner might begin by introducing the dog to a few calm and friendly people in a quiet environment. As the dog becomes more comfortable, it can be gradually introduced to busier and more challenging environments, such as a park or a crowded street. This gradual approach helps the dog build confidence and learn to handle various situations calmly and appropriately.

In the context of positive reinforcement training, consistency and patience are crucial for ensuring that the training methods are effective and humane. Positive reinforcement relies on rewarding desired behaviors, and for this to be effective, the rewards must be consistent and timely. If the rewards are inconsistent or delayed, the dog may not make the connection between the behavior and the reward, which can hinder learning.

Consistency in positive reinforcement also involves using the same rewards and praise for the same behaviors. If the dog receives different rewards for the same behavior, it may become confused about what is expected. Using consistent rewards helps the dog understand exactly what behavior is being reinforced.

Patience is also essential when using positive reinforcement. Some behaviors may take longer to learn than others, and it is important to remain patient and persistent. If the dog does not immediately understand what is being asked, the owner should remain calm and continue to reinforce the desired behavior with rewards and praise. Over time, the dog will learn the behavior and the training will be successful.

Consistency and patience are not only important for training and socialization but also for building a strong and trusting relationship between the dog and its owner. Dogs thrive on routine and predictability, and consistent training helps create a sense of security and stability. Patience helps build trust, as the dog learns that the owner is reliable and supportive.

In addition to training sessions, consistency and patience should be applied to all interactions with the dog. For example, feeding times, walk schedules, and playtime should be consistent to create a predictable routine for the dog. Consistency in daily routines helps the dog feel secure and reduces anxiety.

Patience is also important in daily interactions, especially when dealing with challenges or setbacks. Dogs, like humans, have good days and bad days, and it is important to remain patient and understanding. If the dog is having an off day or is not responding well to training, it is better to take a break and try again later rather than becoming frustrated.

In conclusion, consistency and patience are essential principles of successful dog training. Consistency in commands, rewards, and daily routines helps the dog understand what is expected and reinforces desired behaviors. Patience allows the dog time to learn and master new skills and helps build a strong and trusting relationship. By applying these principles, owners can create a positive and effective training environment that fosters a well-behaved and happy dog.

Whether teaching basic commands, addressing behavioral issues, or socializing the dog, consistency and patience ensure that the training process is smooth, effective, and enjoyable for both the dog and the owner. Through these principles, training becomes a rewarding experience that enhances the bond between the dog and its owner, leading to a harmonious and fulfilling relationship.

Setting Boundaries and Rules

Setting boundaries and rules is a fundamental aspect of dog training, essential for maintaining order and harmony in the household. Establishing clear guidelines for acceptable behavior helps dogs understand their limits and expectations, promoting a balanced and respectful relationship between the dog and its owner. This process involves defining specific behaviors that are acceptable and unacceptable, consistently enforcing these rules, and ensuring that all family members are aligned in their approach.

Clear boundaries provide structure and predictability for dogs, which is essential for their sense of security and well-being. Dogs thrive in environments where they understand what is expected of them and where the rules are consistent. For example, if a dog is not allowed on the furniture, this rule should be applied consistently by everyone in the household. Allowing the dog on the furniture sometimes and not at other times can confuse the dog, leading to frustration and behavioral issues.

One of the first steps in setting boundaries is to define the rules clearly. This involves deciding on the behaviors that are acceptable and those that are not. Common boundaries include rules about where the dog is allowed to go in the house, whether it can jump on people, how it should behave during mealtimes, and how it should respond to commands. These rules should be simple, clear, and consistent. For instance, a rule might be that the dog is not allowed in the kitchen while food is being prepared. Enforcing this rule consistently helps the dog understand its boundaries and what is expected.

Consistency in enforcing rules is crucial. If a dog is allowed to break a rule occasionally, it will not understand the importance of following the rule. This inconsistency can lead to confusion and make training more difficult. For example, if a dog is allowed to beg for food at the table sometimes but is scolded for it at other times, it will not understand that begging is unacceptable. Consistently enforcing the rule every time the dog begs helps reinforce the behavior that is expected.

Positive reinforcement is a powerful tool for setting boundaries. Rewarding the dog for following rules and behaving appropriately helps reinforce the desired behavior. For example, if the rule is that the dog should sit quietly while the family eats, rewarding the dog with a treat or praise when it sits quietly reinforces this behavior. Positive reinforcement helps the dog understand that following the rules leads to positive outcomes, making it more likely to repeat the behavior.

Another important aspect of setting boundaries is to ensure that all family members are on the same page. Consistency in enforcing rules by everyone in the household is essential for the dog to understand and follow the rules. If one person allows the dog to jump on the couch while another does not, the dog receives mixed signals, making it difficult to learn the rules. Family meetings to discuss and agree on the rules can help ensure consistency and avoid confusion.

Setting boundaries also involves teaching the dog to respect personal space. This is particularly important in households with small children or elderly family members who may be more vulnerable to being knocked over or startled by an enthusiastic dog. Teaching the dog to wait for an invitation before jumping on people, or to stay out of certain areas of the house, helps establish respect for personal space and reduces the risk of accidents.

Boundaries are not only important inside the house but also outside. For example, setting boundaries about how the dog should behave during walks is essential. Teaching the dog to walk calmly on a leash, not to pull, and to respond to commands like "heel" and "stay" helps ensure safe and enjoyable walks. Consistent enforcement of these rules during every walk reinforces the behavior and helps the dog understand what is expected.

Another critical aspect of setting boundaries is teaching the dog to respect other animals and people. This involves socialization and training to ensure the dog behaves appropriately around other dogs, cats, and people. For example, teaching the dog not to chase or bark at other animals, and to greet people calmly, helps establish boundaries and promotes positive interactions. Socialization should be done gradually and in a controlled manner, with positive reinforcement used to reward appropriate behavior.

Setting boundaries also involves managing the dog's environment to prevent unwanted behavior. For example, if a dog tends to chew on shoes, keeping shoes out of reach and providing appropriate chew toys helps prevent the behavior. Managing the environment to prevent access to temptations makes it easier for the dog to follow the rules and reinforces the boundaries that have been set.

Boundaries should be established from an early age. Puppies are like sponges, absorbing information and learning quickly. Establishing clear rules and boundaries from the beginning helps puppies understand what is expected and prevents the development of undesirable behaviors. Early training and socialization are crucial for setting a solid foundation for future behavior.

However, it is important to be patient and understanding when setting boundaries, especially with puppies and rescue dogs who may have had little training in the past. These dogs may need more time to learn and adapt to the rules. Consistent reinforcement, positive reinforcement, and patience are key to helping these dogs understand and follow the boundaries.

In summary, setting boundaries and rules is an essential aspect of dog training that helps maintain order and harmony in the household. Clear and consistent boundaries provide structure and predictability, which are crucial for a dog's sense of security and well-being. Positive reinforcement helps reinforce desired behaviors, making it more likely that the dog will follow the rules. Ensuring that all family members are consistent in enforcing the rules prevents confusion and promotes effective training. Managing the dog's environment and being patient and understanding during the training process also contribute to successful boundary setting. By establishing clear boundaries and rules, owners can create a harmonious and balanced environment that fosters a well-behaved and happy dog.

Setting boundaries and rules not only helps in training but also enhances the bond between the dog and its owner, leading to a more fulfilling and enjoyable relationship.

CHAPTER 4

PUPPY TRAINING

Puppy training is the essential process of teaching your new puppy basic commands, social skills, and acceptable behaviors. Starting early helps shape your puppy into a well-behaved and confident adult dog. Key aspects of puppy training include housebreaking, socialization, and teaching basic commands like "sit," "stay," and "come." Using positive reinforcement techniques and maintaining consistency and patience throughout the training ensures that your puppy learns effectively and enjoys the process. This early training not only promotes good behavior but also strengthens the bond between you and your puppy.

Housebreaking and Crate Training

Housebreaking and crate training are fundamental aspects of raising a well-behaved and content German Shepherd. These processes not only teach the dog where and when it is appropriate to relieve itself but also provide it with a sense of security and a safe space to retreat to. Properly housebreaking and crate training a German Shepherd requires patience, consistency, and a clear understanding of the dog's natural behaviors and instincts.

Housebreaking, also known as potty training, involves teaching a dog to eliminate outside or in a designated area rather than inside the house. One of the most effective methods to housebreak a German Shepherd is to establish a consistent routine. Taking the dog outside at the same times each day—such as first thing in the morning, after meals, and before bed—helps the dog learn when and where it should go to the bathroom. Dogs thrive on routine, and a consistent schedule helps reinforce the desired behavior.

A German Shepherd puppy being taken outside early in the morning for its first bathroom break of the day.

Another critical aspect of housebreaking is positive reinforcement. When the dog eliminates in the appropriate spot, immediately rewarding it with praise, a treat, or playtime reinforces the behavior. Positive reinforcement helps the dog make a connection between eliminating outside and receiving a reward, making it more likely to repeat the behavior in the future.

Supervision is crucial during the initial stages of housebreaking. Keeping a close eye on the dog and looking for signs that it needs to go outside, such as sniffing around or circling, can prevent accidents inside the house. If an accident does occur, it is important to clean the area thoroughly to remove any odors that might attract the dog to the same spot again. Avoiding punishment is essential, as scolding a dog after an accident can create fear and confusion, hindering the training process.

Crate training complements housebreaking and provides the dog with a safe and comfortable space. Dogs have a natural instinct to keep their sleeping area clean, so they are less likely to eliminate in their crate if it is the right size. The crate should be large enough for the dog to stand, turn around, and lie down comfortably but not so large that it can use one end as a bathroom and the other as a sleeping area.

A German Shepherd puppy comfortably lying in a properly sized crate with a soft blanket and a chew toy.

Introducing the crate gradually is important to ensure the dog feels safe and secure. Start by placing treats and toys inside the crate and encouraging the dog to explore it voluntarily. Once the dog is comfortable, begin closing the door for short periods while staying nearby. Gradually increase the time the dog spends in the crate, always making sure it has positive associations with the space. Feeding the dog its meals in the crate can also help create a positive connection.

Using the crate effectively involves timing and consistency. The dog should be placed in the crate during designated times, such as bedtime or when the owner is away for short periods. Consistently taking the dog outside immediately after releasing it from the crate helps reinforce the idea that eliminating should happen outside. The crate should never be used as a form of punishment, as this can create negative associations and increase anxiety.

As the dog becomes more reliable with housebreaking, the amount of time it spends in the crate can be gradually reduced. The goal is for the crate to become a place the dog willingly goes to for comfort and security, not a place of confinement. Some dogs may even choose to sleep in their crate with the door open once they have developed a positive association with it.

Housebreaking and crate training are foundational elements of a well-behaved dog. By using consistent routines, positive reinforcement, and gradual acclimatization, German Shepherds can learn to eliminate appropriately and view their crate as a safe haven. These training methods not only prevent accidents and destructive behaviors but also enhance the bond between the dog and its owner.

Socialization with People and Other Animals

Socialization is a critical component of raising a German Shepherd, as it helps the dog develop into a well-adjusted and confident adult. Proper socialization involves exposing the dog to a variety of people, animals, environments, and experiences in a controlled and positive manner. This process is essential for preventing fear and aggression and for ensuring that the dog can interact safely and comfortably in different situations.

Early socialization should begin as soon as the puppy arrives home. Introducing the German Shepherd to a variety of people, including men, women, children, and people of different ethnicities and ages, helps the dog become comfortable with diverse human interactions. Positive experiences with a range of individuals reduce the likelihood of fear-based aggression and help the dog develop into a friendly and confident adult.

A German Shepherd puppy being gently petted and praised by a group of children in a park.

Exposing the dog to different environments is equally important. Taking the dog to parks, pet-friendly stores, and urban areas helps it adapt to various sights, sounds, and smells. Gradually increasing the level of stimulation in these environments helps prevent sensory overload and ensures the dog remains calm and focused. Positive reinforcement, such as treats and praise, should be used to reward calm and appropriate behavior in new settings.

Socializing the dog with other animals is another crucial aspect. Controlled introductions to other dogs, cats, and even smaller pets like rabbits or birds can help the dog learn to interact peacefully with different species. Dog parks and puppy play-dates provide opportunities for the dog to practice social skills in a safe and supervised environment. It is important to monitor these interactions closely and intervene if any signs of aggression or fear appear.

A German Shepherd puppy playing amicably with other puppies in a dog park under the supervision of their owners.

Socialization should be a positive experience for the dog. Using rewards, such as treats, toys, and praise, helps reinforce good behavior and makes social interactions enjoyable. Short, frequent socialization sessions are more effective than long, overwhelming ones. If the dog shows signs of stress or fear, it is important to remove it from the situation and try again later, gradually increasing exposure as the dog's confidence grows.

Training classes offer structured socialization opportunities. Puppy classes provide a controlled environment where the dog can interact with other puppies and people under the guidance of a professional trainer. These classes not only help with socialization but also teach basic obedience skills and proper play behavior.

Socialization is not limited to the puppy stage; it should continue throughout the dog's life. Regular exposure to new people, animals, and environments helps maintain the dog's social skills and adaptability. Adult dogs that were well-socialized as puppies tend to handle new experiences and changes more easily, reducing the risk of behavioral issues.

Proper socialization helps prevent behavioral problems such as fear aggression, anxiety, and excessive barking. Well-socialized dogs are more likely to be friendly, confident, and well-behaved in various situations, making them enjoyable companions. This positive behavior enhances the dog's quality of life and ensures that it can safely and comfortably interact with the world around it.

Basic Commands: Sit, Stay, Come

Teaching basic commands like "sit," "stay," and "come" is fundamental for a well-mannered and obedient German Shepherd. These commands not only enhance the dog's behavior but also ensure its safety and strengthen the bond between the dog and its owner. Training should be conducted using positive reinforcement techniques, ensuring that learning is a positive and rewarding experience for the dog.

The "sit" command is often the first command taught because it is simple and forms the foundation for more complex behaviors. To teach "sit," hold a treat close to the dog's nose and slowly move it upward. As the dog's head follows the treat, its bottom will naturally lower to the ground. Once the dog is in the sitting position, say "sit" and immediately reward it with the treat and praise. Repeating this process several times in short sessions helps the dog understand the command.

A German Shepherd puppy sitting obediently while its owner holds a treat just above its nose, demonstrating the "sit" command.

The "stay" command builds on the "sit" command and teaches the dog impulse control. Start by asking the dog to sit. Once it is sitting, hold your hand out, palm facing the dog, and say "stay" while taking a step back. If the dog remains in place, immediately reward it with a treat and praise. Gradually increase the distance and duration before giving the reward, always returning to the dog to reward it for staying. If the dog breaks the stay, calmly guide it back to the original position and try again. Consistency and patience are key to teaching a reliable "stay."

A German Shepherd holding the "stay" position while its owner takes a few steps back, ready to reward the dog for maintaining the stay.

The "come" command, or recall, is one of the most important commands for the dog's safety. Start training "come" in a quiet, distraction-free environment. Using a long leash, let the dog explore a bit, then gently tug the leash while enthusiastically saying "come." When the dog comes to you, reward it with a treat and lots of praise. Practice this command in different locations and gradually introduce more distractions. A strong recall command ensures that the dog returns to you immediately, which can prevent it from running into dangerous situations.

A German Shepherd running eagerly towards its owner in response to the "come" command, demonstrating a strong recall.

Positive reinforcement is essential for teaching these commands. Rewards, such as treats, toys, and praise, motivate the dog to learn and obey commands. Training sessions should be short and frequent to keep the dog engaged and prevent frustration. Consistency in using the same commands and hand signals helps the dog understand what is expected.

Training should be a positive experience for the dog. Using a calm and encouraging tone of voice, along with plenty of praise and rewards, makes training enjoyable and strengthens the bond between the dog and its owner. Avoiding punishment and negative reinforcement ensures that the dog remains confident and willing to learn.

Training classes can be beneficial for teaching basic commands. Professional trainers can provide guidance and support, helping owners effectively teach their dogs. Classes also offer opportunities for socialization and practicing commands in a controlled environment with distractions.

Incorporating training into daily routines reinforces commands and makes them part of the dog's normal behavior. Asking the dog to sit before meals, stay while the door is opened, or come during playtime helps reinforce the commands and ensures that the dog understands and obeys them in various situations.

Basic commands like "sit," "stay," and "come" are essential for a well-behaved and obedient dog. Teaching these commands using positive reinforcement techniques ensures that the dog learns in a positive and enjoyable manner. Consistent practice and incorporating commands into daily routines help reinforce the behavior and ensure that the dog responds reliably.

Well-trained dogs are not only safer and easier to manage but also more confident and happy, enhancing the quality of life for both the dog and its owner.

CHAPTER 5

ADVANCED TRAINING

Advanced training for German Shepherds elevates their obedience and social skills, enabling them to perform more complex tasks and commands. This stage involves refining basic skills, introducing new commands, and ensuring reliability both on and off the leash. Advanced training not only enhances the dog's abilities but also provides mental stimulation, which is crucial for this intelligent and active breed. By progressing to advanced training, owners can expect their dogs to be more responsive and adaptable in various situations, further strengthening their bond and ensuring the dog's safety and well-being.

Leash Training and Walking on a Lead

Leash training is a fundamental aspect of a dog's training regimen. For German Shepherds, who are known for their strength and energy, learning to walk calmly on a leash is crucial. Proper leash training ensures that walks are enjoyable and safe for both the dog and the owner. This process requires patience, consistency, and positive reinforcement to achieve the best results.

The first step in leash training is selecting the right equipment. A sturdy leash and a comfortable, well-fitting collar or harness are essential. For German Shepherds, a harness can be particularly beneficial as it distributes pressure more evenly across the dog's body, reducing the risk of injury and giving the owner better control.

A German Shepherd wearing a comfortable harness, standing calmly beside its owner on a well-fitted leash in a park.

Before beginning outdoor leash training, it is beneficial to start indoors where there are fewer distractions. Attach the leash to the dog's collar or harness and let it drag the leash around to get used to the sensation. Encourage the dog to follow you around the house, rewarding it with treats and praise for staying close and walking without pulling.

Once the dog is comfortable with the leash indoors, it's time to transition to outdoor training. Start in a quiet, low-distraction environment such as your backyard. Begin walking with the dog, holding the leash firmly but not tightly. If the dog starts to pull, stop walking immediately. Wait for the dog to return to your side or to stop pulling before continuing. This teaches the dog that pulling on the leash will not get it where it wants to go.

Positive reinforcement is key in leash training. Whenever the dog walks calmly beside you, reward it with treats, praise, and affection. This reinforces the idea that walking by your side is a desirable behavior. Consistency is crucial; ensure that every member of the household follows the same rules and techniques to avoid confusing the dog.

As the dog becomes more adept at walking calmly on a leash, gradually introduce more distractions, such as other people, dogs, and busy environments. It is important to remain patient and consistent, rewarding good behavior and calmly correcting undesirable behavior. If the dog becomes overly excited or distracted, redirect its attention back to you with a treat or a toy.

Leash training also involves teaching the dog specific commands that make walking easier and safer. Commands like "heel," "sit," and "wait" are particularly useful. The "heel" command instructs the dog to walk closely beside you, which is essential in crowded or potentially hazardous situations. To teach "heel," start walking and use a treat to guide the dog to your side. Once the dog is in position, say "heel" and reward it. Practice this consistently until the dog reliably walks beside you on command.

A German Shepherd walking calmly beside its owner on a leash, maintaining the "heel" position in a busy park.

Teaching the dog to "sit" at intersections or when stopping for any reason ensures that it remains under control and prevents it from lunging or pulling. The "wait" command is useful for keeping the dog still when you need to attend to something or when crossing the street. Consistently using these commands during walks reinforces the dog's training and ensures that walks remain controlled and pleasant.

Leash training is an ongoing process. Regular practice and reinforcement are necessary to maintain the dog's skills and ensure that it remains responsive to commands. Advanced leash training may include practicing in different environments and gradually increasing the duration and complexity of walks. This helps the dog remain adaptable and well-behaved in various situations.

Leash training a German Shepherd requires patience, consistency, and positive reinforcement. By starting indoors, transitioning to outdoor training, and gradually introducing distractions, owners can teach their dogs to walk calmly and safely on a leash. Incorporating specific commands like "heel," "sit," and "wait" further enhances the dog's control and responsiveness, making walks enjoyable and safe for both the dog and the owner.

Off-Leash Training

Off-leash training is a crucial aspect of advanced obedience for German Shepherds. It allows the dog to explore and exercise freely while maintaining control and ensuring safety. Successful off-leash training relies on a solid foundation of basic obedience, reliable recall, and trust between the dog and its owner.

Before beginning off-leash training, it is essential that the dog has mastered basic commands such as "sit," "stay," and, most importantly, "come." A reliable recall command ensures that the dog will return to its owner immediately, even in the presence of distractions. Off-leash training should start in a secure, fenced area where the dog cannot run off or encounter dangers.

A German Shepherd running freely in a large, fenced yard, responding to its owner's recall command.

Begin by allowing the dog to explore the fenced area while carrying a long training leash. This leash gives the dog a sense of freedom while allowing the owner to maintain control if needed. Periodically call the dog back using the recall command. When the dog returns, reward it with treats, praise, and affection. This reinforces the behavior and encourages the dog to respond reliably.

Gradually increase the distance between the dog and the owner during recall training. Practice calling the dog back from various distances and distractions, always rewarding successful recalls. Consistency and positive reinforcement are key to building a reliable recall. If the dog does not respond immediately, avoid punishment and instead use a more enticing reward or a playful tone to encourage it.

Once the dog demonstrates reliable recall in a secure area, progress to more open environments. Start with quiet, low-distraction areas such as an empty field or a secluded park. Gradually introduce more distractions, such as other dogs, people, and wildlife. The goal is for the dog to respond to the recall command regardless of the surrounding environment.

Using a high-value reward, such as a favorite treat or toy, can help reinforce the recall command in more challenging situations. Practice regularly and vary the training locations to ensure that the dog remains responsive in different settings. Off-leash training should always be conducted in safe environments where the dog is not at risk of running into traffic or other hazards.

Teaching the dog to check in with its owner periodically is another important aspect of off-leash training. Encourage the dog to return to the owner frequently, even without being called. Reward these check-ins to reinforce the behavior and ensure that the dog remains aware of its owner's location.

A German Shepherd checking in with its owner during an off-leash walk in a forested area.

In addition to recall, teaching the dog to respond to other commands off-leash is essential for maintaining control. Commands such as "sit," "stay," and "leave it" help manage the dog's behavior in various situations. Practice these commands regularly during off-leash training sessions, rewarding compliance and reinforcing the dog's obedience.

Off-leash training is an ongoing process that requires regular practice and reinforcement. Maintaining a strong bond with the dog and using positive reinforcement techniques ensures that the dog remains responsive and well-behaved. Advanced off-leash training provides the dog with the freedom to explore while ensuring its safety and control.

Off-leash training offers numerous benefits for both the dog and its owner. It allows the dog to exercise and explore more freely, which is particularly important for active breeds like German Shepherds. It also enhances the dog's mental stimulation and confidence. For the owner, off-leash training provides greater convenience and peace of mind, knowing that the dog can be trusted to respond reliably in various situations.

Successful off-leash training hinges on a strong foundation of basic obedience, reliable recall, and consistent practice. By starting in secure environments and gradually introducing more challenging settings, owners can teach their German Shepherds to enjoy the freedom of off-leash exploration while maintaining control and ensuring safety.

Advanced Commands: Heel, Down, Leave It

Advanced commands are crucial for enhancing a German Shepherd's obedience and ensuring that it remains well-behaved in various situations. Commands such as "heel," "down," and "leave it" build on basic obedience training and help manage the dog's behavior more effectively.

The "heel" command is essential for controlling the dog during walks, particularly in busy or potentially hazardous environments. To teach "heel," start with the dog on a leash. Hold a treat in your hand and position it at your side, close to your leg. Begin walking and use the treat to guide the dog into position beside you. Once the dog is walking calmly by your side, say "heel" and reward it with the treat. Practice this consistently, gradually increasing the duration and difficulty by introducing distractions.

The "down" command is useful for managing the dog's behavior in various situations, such as when guests arrive or when the dog needs to settle. To teach "down," start with the dog in a sitting position. Hold a treat in your hand and slowly lower it to the ground, guiding the dog's nose to follow. As the dog's front legs lower to the ground, say "down" and reward it with the treat.

Practice this regularly, gradually increasing the duration the dog remains in the down position before rewarding.

The "leave it" command is essential for ensuring the dog's safety and preventing it from picking up or approaching unwanted objects. To teach "leave it," start with a treat in both hands. Show the dog one treat and then close your hand around it. When the dog tries to get the treat, say "leave it" and wait for the dog to stop trying. Once the dog backs away or looks away, reward it with the treat from your other hand. Practice this regularly, gradually introducing more tempting objects and increasing the difficulty.

A German Shepherd being taught the "leave it" command with a tempting treat placed nearby.

Advanced commands require consistent practice and positive reinforcement to ensure that the dog responds reliably. Regular training sessions, incorporating these commands into daily routines, and gradually increasing the difficulty help reinforce the behavior and ensure that the dog remains obedient in various situations.

Training a German Shepherd to respond to advanced commands like "heel," "down," and "leave it" enhances its obedience and control. These commands are essential for managing the dog's behavior in different environments and ensuring its safety. Using positive reinforcement techniques, such as treats, praise, and play, makes the learning process enjoyable for the dog and encourages it to repeat desired behaviors.

Advanced training provides numerous benefits for both the dog and its owner. For the dog, it offers mental stimulation and the opportunity to learn and perform more complex tasks. For the owner, it ensures that the dog remains well-behaved and responsive, enhancing the quality of life for both. Regular practice and reinforcement are key to maintaining the dog's skills and ensuring that it continues to respond reliably to advanced commands.

By teaching advanced commands, owners can ensure that their German Shepherds remain well-behaved and under control in various situations. This training enhances the dog's obedience, mental stimulation, and overall well-being, contributing to a happy and harmonious relationship between the dog and its owner.

CHAPTER 6
Behavioral Issues and Solutions

Addressing Common Behavioral Problems

Behavioral problems in dogs can arise due to a variety of factors, including genetics, lack of training, or insufficient socialization. For German Shepherds, a highly intelligent and active breed, addressing these issues early on is crucial to prevent them from becoming ingrained habits. Effective strategies involve understanding the root causes and employing consistent training and positive reinforcement.

One common behavioral problem is excessive barking. German Shepherds are naturally vocal, but excessive barking can become problematic. Identifying the cause is the first step—whether it's boredom, anxiety, or a reaction to external stimuli. Providing ample physical and mental stimulation can reduce boredom-related barking. Engaging toys, regular exercise, and training sessions can keep the dog occupied. For anxiety-induced barking, desensitization techniques and creating a calm environment can be beneficial. Training the dog to understand the "quiet" command, using treats and praise, helps manage barking triggered by excitement or environmental changes.

A German Shepherd playing with a puzzle toy to reduce boredom-induced barking.

Digging is another common behavior that can be problematic. Dogs dig for various reasons including boredom, instinct, or to cool off. Providing a designated digging area, such as a sandbox, can redirect this natural behavior. Encouraging the dog to use the designated area by burying toys or treats can make it more appealing. Additionally, ensuring the dog has plenty of physical and mental exercise can reduce the likelihood of digging out of boredom.

Chewing is a natural behavior for dogs, but it becomes problematic when they chew on inappropriate objects like furniture, shoes, or other household items. Providing a variety of appropriate chew toys can help satisfy the dog's need to chew. Rotating the toys to keep them interesting and using toys that can be stuffed with treats or peanut butter can keep the dog engaged. If the dog chews on inappropriate objects, redirecting it to the appropriate toys and using deterrent sprays on household items can be effective strategies.

Jumping on people is a common issue, especially in young, energetic dogs. This behavior is often a result of excitement and a desire for attention. Teaching the dog an alternative behavior, such as sitting or greeting people calmly, can help manage this issue. Consistently rewarding the dog for keeping all four paws on the ground and ignoring it when it jumps can reinforce the desired behavior. Ensuring that everyone who interacts with the dog follows the same approach is crucial for consistency.

A German Shepherd sitting calmly and receiving a treat for greeting a visitor without jumping.

Addressing common behavioral problems requires patience, consistency, and an understanding of the underlying causes. Providing appropriate outlets for natural behaviors, ensuring sufficient physical and mental stimulation, and using positive reinforcement techniques can help guide dogs toward more appropriate behaviors.

Dealing with Aggression and Fear

Aggression and fear are serious behavioral issues that require careful management and training. Understanding the root causes of these behaviors is essential for effectively addressing them. Aggression can be caused by fear, territoriality, resource guarding, or lack of socialization. Fear can result from past trauma, lack of exposure to various stimuli, or genetic predisposition. Addressing these issues involves a combination of behavior modification techniques, training, and in some cases, professional intervention.

Aggression often stems from fear or anxiety. When a dog feels threatened, it may resort to aggressive behaviors as a defense mechanism. Identifying and addressing the triggers of fear or anxiety is the first step in managing aggression. Gradual desensitization and counterconditioning can help reduce the dog's fear response to specific triggers. This involves exposing the dog to the trigger at a low intensity and pairing it with positive experiences such as treats or play. Over time, the dog learns to associate the trigger with positive outcomes rather than fear or aggression.

Resource guarding is another common cause of aggression. This occurs when a dog becomes aggressive over food, toys, or other valued items. Teaching the dog to "drop it" or "leave it" and rewarding it for relinquishing items can help manage this behavior. Gradual desensitization exercises, such as hand-feeding or trading a valued item for a high-value treat, can also reduce resource guarding tendencies.

Socialization plays a critical role in preventing and managing aggression and fear. Exposing the dog to a variety of people, animals, and environments in a controlled and positive manner can help it develop confidence and reduce fear-based aggression. Socialization should be done gradually, ensuring that the dog is not overwhelmed and that each experience is positive.

Professional help from a veterinarian or a certified animal behaviorist may be necessary for severe cases of aggression and fear. A thorough assessment can help determine the underlying causes and develop a tailored behavior modification plan. In some cases, medication may be recommended to help manage anxiety or fear while training and behavior modification are implemented.

Fear can manifest in various ways, including cowering, trembling, excessive barking, or aggression. Identifying the specific triggers of fear and working to desensitize the dog to these triggers is essential. Creating a safe and calm environment, using calming aids, and providing positive reinforcement for calm behavior can help reduce fear responses. Gradual exposure to fear-inducing stimuli, combined with positive reinforcement, helps the dog build confidence and reduce fear over time.

Managing aggression and fear requires a comprehensive approach that includes understanding the root causes, implementing behavior modification techniques, and providing positive reinforcement. With patience, consistency, and professional guidance when needed, it is possible to help dogs overcome these challenging behaviors and lead happier, more confident lives.

Managing Separation Anxiety

Separation anxiety is a common behavioral issue in dogs that occurs when they become overly anxious or distressed when left alone. This can lead to destructive behaviors, excessive barking, and other signs of distress. Managing separation anxiety involves creating a positive association with being alone, gradually increasing the time the dog spends alone, and providing mental and physical stimulation to reduce anxiety.

Creating a positive association with being alone is the first step in managing separation anxiety. This can be achieved by providing special toys or treats that the dog only receives when left alone. Puzzle toys, treat-dispensing toys, or stuffed Kongs can keep the dog occupied and provide a positive distraction. Ensuring that the dog has a comfortable and safe space, such as a crate or a designated area, can also help reduce anxiety.

A German Shepherd happily engaged with a puzzle toy in a comfortable, designated area.

Gradually increasing the time the dog spends alone helps it build tolerance to being left alone. Start by leaving the dog alone for short periods, gradually increasing the duration as the dog becomes more comfortable. During this process, avoid making a big fuss when leaving or returning home, as this can heighten the dog's anxiety. Instead, keep departures and arrivals low-key to help the dog remain calm.

Providing mental and physical stimulation can help reduce separation anxiety by tiring the dog out and keeping it occupied. Regular exercise, interactive toys, and training sessions can help expend excess energy and reduce anxiety. Ensuring that the dog receives plenty of attention and interaction when the owner is home can also help alleviate separation anxiety.

Training the dog to remain calm and relaxed in the owner's absence is an important part of managing separation anxiety. Start by teaching the dog to settle in its designated area while the owner is still at home. Gradually increase the distance between the dog and the owner, rewarding the dog for remaining calm and relaxed. Over time, the dog learns to associate the designated area with calmness and security.

In some cases, professional help from a veterinarian or a certified animal behaviorist may be necessary. They can provide guidance on developing a tailored behavior modification plan and recommend strategies or medications to help manage anxiety. Calming aids, such as pheromone diffusers or anxiety wraps, can also be beneficial in reducing anxiety.

Separation anxiety can be challenging to manage, but with patience, consistency, and a comprehensive approach, it is possible to help dogs overcome this issue. Creating positive associations with being alone, gradually increasing the time spent alone, and providing mental and physical stimulation can help reduce anxiety and destructive behaviors. Professional guidance and support can also be valuable in managing more severe cases of separation anxiety.

Addressing common behavioral problems, managing aggression and fear, and dealing with separation anxiety are essential aspects of responsible dog ownership. Understanding the root causes, implementing effective training and behavior modification techniques, and providing positive reinforcement can help dogs develop appropriate behaviors and lead happier, more confident lives. With patience, consistency, and professional support when needed, owners can successfully manage these challenging behaviors and enjoy a harmonious relationship with their dogs.

CHAPTER 7

Specialized Training

Guard and Protection Training

Guard and protection training for dogs, particularly breeds like German Shepherds, requires a structured and professional approach to ensure the dog performs its duties effectively and safely. This type of training involves teaching the dog to recognize potential threats, protect its handler or property, and respond to commands under high-stress situations. It is essential to begin with a solid foundation of obedience training before moving on to more advanced protection tasks.

A German Shepherd attentively watching its handler during a training session

The first step in guard and protection training is to instill strong obedience skills. The dog must be able to follow basic commands such as sit, stay, come, and heel without hesitation. These commands form the basis for more advanced training and ensure that the dog is under control at all times. Consistency and positive reinforcement are key during this phase to build a reliable and trustworthy relationship between the dog and handler.

Once a solid obedience foundation is established, the next phase involves introducing the dog to protection work. This often begins with teaching the dog to bark on command and to alert the handler to the presence of a stranger or potential threat. Using positive reinforcement, such as treats or praise, the dog is encouraged to bark and then quiet down when commanded. This controlled barking is crucial for signaling an intruder's presence without escalating to aggressive behavior prematurely.

A German Shepherd practicing the bark on command during a protection training session.

After mastering alert barking, the dog is trained to protect its handler and property. This involves bite training, where the dog learns to apprehend a potential threat on command. Professional trainers use bite sleeves and suits to teach the dog how to bite and hold an intruder without causing unnecessary harm. The emphasis is on control and precision, ensuring the dog only bites when commanded and releases on cue. This phase of training requires a high level of expertise to prevent the development of uncontrolled aggression.

In addition to bite training, the dog is taught to remain calm and composed in high-stress situations. Desensitization exercises expose the dog to various distractions, loud noises, and chaotic environments to ensure it can focus on its duties without becoming overwhelmed. The goal is to develop a dog that is confident, composed, and capable of making quick, decisive actions to protect its handler and property.

A German Shepherd undergoing bite training with a professional trainer wearing a protective suit.

Proper guard and protection training also involves socialization and ensuring the dog can differentiate between real threats and benign situations. The dog must be able to interact peacefully with family members, guests, and other animals while remaining vigilant. This balance is achieved through ongoing training and reinforcement, emphasizing the importance of obedience and control.

Advanced protection training may also include scenario-based exercises, where the dog and handler practice responding to simulated threats. These exercises help the dog develop situational awareness and reinforce the handler's ability to give clear, concise commands under pressure. Regular training sessions and continued practice are essential to maintain the dog's skills and readiness.

Guard and protection training transforms a well-trained dog into a reliable protector capable of responding to potential threats while remaining under control. This specialized training enhances the dog's natural guarding instincts and ensures it can perform its duties effectively and safely. By focusing on obedience, controlled aggression, and ongoing practice, handlers can develop a dog that is both a loyal companion and a formidable guardian.

Search and Rescue Training

Search and rescue (SAR) training harnesses a dog's natural abilities to locate and assist in finding missing persons. Breeds like German Shepherds are particularly well-suited for this type of work due to their intelligence, agility, and strong work ethic. SAR training involves teaching the dog to use its keen sense of smell and tracking instincts to locate individuals in various environments and conditions.

The first step in SAR training is to develop the dog's scent detection skills. This involves introducing the dog to different scents and teaching it to associate specific scents with finding a person. Using positive reinforcement, such as treats and praise, the dog learns to focus on the target scent and follow it to its source. Training exercises often start with simple scent trails and gradually increase in complexity as the dog becomes more proficient.

A German Shepherd practicing scent detection during a search and rescue training session.

Once the dog has mastered basic scent detection, it is introduced to more challenging environments. SAR dogs must be able to work in diverse settings, including forests, urban areas, and disaster sites. Training sessions are conducted in different locations to ensure the dog can adapt to various terrains and conditions. These exercises help the dog develop the ability to navigate obstacles, search through debris, and maintain focus in chaotic environments.

In addition to scent detection, SAR training involves teaching the dog to alert its handler when it has found a person. This can be achieved through different methods, such as barking, returning to the handler and leading them to the location, or using a specific signal like a trained behavior. Consistent reinforcement and practice are essential to ensure the dog reliably performs the alert behavior.

A German Shepherd alerting its handler after locating a person during a search and rescue exercise.

Training for SAR also includes developing the dog's endurance and physical fitness. SAR dogs often work for extended periods in challenging conditions, so maintaining their physical health is crucial. Regular exercise, conditioning, and veterinary check-ups are essential components of a SAR dog's training regimen.

Socialization and teamwork are also critical in SAR training. The dog must be able to work effectively with its handler and other SAR team members. Building a strong bond between the dog and handler through regular training and interaction ensures effective communication and cooperation during search missions. The dog must also be comfortable working alongside other dogs and responders without becoming distracted or stressed.

Advanced SAR training includes scenario-based exercises that simulate real-life search missions. These scenarios help the dog and handler practice their skills in a controlled environment, preparing them for actual deployments. Exercises may involve searching for hidden volunteers, locating scent articles, and navigating complex environments. Regular participation in these exercises ensures the dog remains sharp and ready for real search and rescue operations.

SAR training transforms a dog's natural abilities into lifesaving skills that can make a significant difference in emergency situations. By developing scent detection, alert behaviors, physical fitness, and teamwork, SAR dogs become invaluable assets in locating and rescuing missing persons. The rigorous training and ongoing practice ensure that these dogs are prepared to respond effectively to various search and rescue scenarios.

Therapy and Service Dog Training

Therapy and service dogs provide invaluable assistance and support to individuals with physical, emotional, or mental health challenges. Training these dogs involves teaching them specific skills and behaviors to help their handlers navigate daily life and improve their quality of life. Breeds like German Shepherds are often chosen for these roles due to their intelligence, trainability, and strong bond with humans.

Therapy dogs are trained to provide comfort and companionship to individuals in settings such as hospitals, nursing homes, schools, and disaster areas. The first step in training a therapy dog is to ensure it has a calm and friendly temperament. Socialization is crucial, exposing the dog to different people, environments, and situations to ensure it remains calm and well-behaved in various settings.

In addition to socialization, therapy dogs must learn basic obedience skills and commands to ensure they can respond to their handlers reliably. Commands such as sit, stay, come, and leave it are essential for maintaining control in public spaces. Positive reinforcement techniques, such as treats, praise, and affection, are used to encourage desired behaviors and build a strong bond between the dog and handler.

Therapy dogs must also be comfortable with physical contact and able to remain calm in the presence of medical equipment, loud noises, and other distractions. Training exercises often include visits to different facilities, where the dog can practice interacting with patients and staff, navigating busy environments, and providing comfort through its presence.

Service dogs are trained to perform specific tasks that assist individuals with disabilities. These tasks can include guiding the visually impaired, alerting to sounds for the hearing impaired, retrieving items, providing mobility support, and recognizing and responding to medical conditions such as seizures or low blood sugar. Service dog training is more specialized and tailored to the individual needs of the handler.

The training process for service dogs begins with basic obedience and socialization, similar to therapy dogs. However, service dogs undergo additional task-specific training to meet the unique needs of their handlers. This training often involves breaking down tasks into smaller, manageable steps and using positive reinforcement to teach each step. For example, a service dog may be trained to retrieve items by first learning to touch the item with its nose, then picking it up, and finally bringing it to the handler.

A German Shepherd retrieving an item for its handler as part of service dog training.

Service dogs must also learn to remain focused and perform tasks reliably in various environments, including public spaces, workplaces, and homes. Desensitization exercises help the dog become accustomed to different stimuli and maintain focus on its tasks despite distractions. This level of training requires consistency, patience, and a deep understanding of the handler's needs.

In addition to task-specific training, service dogs must undergo public access training to ensure they can behave appropriately in public settings. This includes walking calmly on a leash, ignoring distractions, and remaining well-behaved in crowded or busy environments. Public access training is crucial for ensuring that the service dog can accompany its handler wherever they go and provide the necessary assistance without causing disruptions.

Both therapy and service dog training require a significant investment of time, effort, and resources. The outcome, however, is a highly trained dog capable of providing essential support and companionship to individuals in need. The benefits of therapy and service dogs extend beyond their handlers, positively impacting the lives of those they interact with daily.

Therapy and service dog training transform intelligent, capable dogs into invaluable partners that enhance the quality of life for individuals with various needs. Through rigorous training, socialization, and task-specific exercises, these dogs develop the skills and behaviors necessary to provide comfort, assistance, and independence to their handlers. The bond between a therapy or service dog and its handler is a testament to the profound impact that these remarkable animals can have on human lives.

CHAPTER 8
Exercise and Enrichment

Physical Exercise Needs

Physical exercise is essential for maintaining the health and well-being of dogs, particularly high-energy breeds like German Shepherds. Regular exercise helps prevent obesity, strengthens muscles, supports cardiovascular health, and reduces behavioral issues caused by pent-up energy. Understanding and meeting the physical exercise needs of a German Shepherd is crucial for ensuring a happy and well-adjusted pet.

German Shepherds are known for their high energy levels and need ample opportunities to run, play, and explore. These dogs were originally bred for herding and working, which means they have a natural inclination for physical activity and thrive on regular exercise. A lack of physical stimulation can lead to destructive behavior, anxiety, and other health problems.

Daily walks are a fundamental part of meeting a German Shepherd's exercise needs. A minimum of two brisk walks per day, each lasting at least 30 to 60 minutes, is recommended. These walks provide an opportunity for physical exercise and mental stimulation as the dog encounters various scents, sights, and sounds in its environment. Varying the walking routes can help keep the dog engaged and excited about its daily outings.

In addition to regular walks, off-leash exercise in a secure, fenced area is highly beneficial for German Shepherds. This allows them to run freely, play fetch, and engage in more vigorous physical activities. Off-leash time is essential for burning off excess energy and providing a sense of freedom and exploration that is crucial for their mental and physical health.

Playing fetch is an excellent way to provide high-intensity exercise for German Shepherds. This activity allows the dog to sprint and retrieve repeatedly, which helps build endurance and muscle strength. Using a ball launcher or other fetching toys can add variety to the game and keep the dog entertained. Additionally, fetch can be played in various environments, such as parks, beaches, or backyards, making it a versatile exercise option.

Another effective way to meet the physical exercise needs of a German Shepherd is through structured activities like agility training. Agility courses involve navigating obstacles such as jumps, tunnels, and weave poles, which challenge the dog's physical abilities and mental acuity. Participating in agility training not only provides intense physical exercise but also strengthens the bond between the dog and its owner through teamwork and communication.

Swimming is an excellent low-impact exercise option for German Shepherds, particularly those with joint issues or arthritis. Swimming provides a full-body workout without putting stress on the joints, making it suitable for dogs of all ages and fitness levels. Many dogs enjoy swimming in lakes, rivers, or pools, and it can be a refreshing way to cool down during hot weather.

Hiking is another great way to provide physical exercise for German Shepherds. Hiking trails offer a variety of terrains and challenges that keep the dog engaged and physically active. The natural environment also provides plenty of mental stimulation as the dog encounters new scents and sights. Hiking can be a shared adventure that promotes bonding and a healthy lifestyle for both the dog and its owner.

A German Shepherd hiking on a forest trail with its owner.

Interactive toys and games that encourage movement, such as tug-of-war, can also help meet a German Shepherd's exercise needs. Tug-of-war engages the dog's natural instincts to pull and shake, providing a fun and interactive way to burn energy. It is important to play tug-of-war with rules to ensure the game remains safe and controlled, such as teaching the dog to release the toy on command.

Ensuring a German Shepherd receives adequate physical exercise is essential for maintaining its overall health and well-being. Regular walks, off-leash play, structured activities like agility training, swimming, hiking, and interactive games all contribute to meeting the exercise needs of this energetic breed. Providing a variety of exercise options keeps the dog engaged, healthy, and happy, preventing behavioral issues and promoting a strong bond between the dog and its owner.

Mental Stimulation and Puzzle Games

Mental stimulation is just as important as physical exercise for maintaining a German Shepherd's overall well-being. This intelligent and highly trainable breed thrives on mental challenges that engage its problem-solving abilities and prevent boredom. Providing a variety of mental stimulation activities, such as puzzle games and interactive toys, can help keep a German Shepherd's mind sharp and satisfied.

Puzzle games are an excellent way to provide mental stimulation for German Shepherds. These games often involve solving a problem to access a reward, such as a treat or toy. There are many types of puzzle games available, ranging from simple treat-dispensing toys to more complex interactive puzzles that require the dog to manipulate pieces to uncover hidden rewards. Puzzle games encourage the dog to use its cognitive skills and provide a sense of accomplishment when the puzzle is solved.

Interactive toys that require the dog to figure out how to release treats are particularly effective for mental stimulation. These toys often involve mechanisms that the dog must learn to manipulate, such as spinning wheels, sliding panels, or pressing buttons. The challenge of figuring out how to access the treats keeps the dog engaged and mentally stimulated, providing a productive outlet for its intelligence and problem-solving abilities.

Training sessions that teach new commands or tricks can also provide valuable mental stimulation. German Shepherds are quick learners and enjoy the challenge of mastering new skills. Regular training sessions that introduce new commands, tricks, or behaviors help keep the dog's mind active and strengthen the bond between the dog and its owner. Using positive reinforcement techniques, such as treats, praise, and play, makes training sessions enjoyable and rewarding for the dog.

Scent work is another excellent way to engage a German Shepherd's mind. Dogs have an incredible sense of smell, and scent work activities tap into this natural ability. Simple scent work games can be created at home by hiding treats or toys around the house or yard and encouraging the dog to find them. More advanced scent work training can involve teaching the dog to identify specific scents or track a scent trail. These activities provide mental stimulation and allow the dog to use its natural instincts in a constructive way.

A German Shepherd participating in a scent work activity, searching for hidden treats.

Rotating toys and activities can help prevent boredom and keep a German Shepherd mentally stimulated. Introducing new toys or changing the environment in which the dog plays can provide fresh challenges and keep the dog's interest. For example, rotating between different puzzle toys, scent work activities, and interactive play sessions can keep the dog engaged and prevent it from becoming bored with its toys and activities.

Interactive play sessions that involve problem-solving can also provide mental stimulation. Games like hide-and-seek, where the owner hides and the dog has to find them, or teaching the dog to pick up and put away its toys, can be both fun and mentally stimulating. These activities encourage the dog to think, follow commands, and use its natural problem-solving abilities in a positive and engaging way.

A German Shepherd playing hide-and-seek with its owner in the backyard.

Incorporating obedience and trick training into daily routines can provide consistent mental challenges. Teaching the dog to perform a series of commands or tricks before receiving a meal, going for a walk, or engaging in playtime can keep its mind active and reinforce positive behaviors. This routine helps the dog understand that mental engagement and following commands are part of its daily life, making it more responsive and well-behaved.

Providing a German Shepherd with a variety of mental stimulation activities is crucial for its overall well-being. Puzzle games, interactive toys, scent work, training sessions, rotating activities, and interactive play sessions all contribute to keeping the dog's mind sharp and engaged. These activities help prevent boredom, reduce behavioral issues, and strengthen the bond between the dog and its owner, ensuring a happy and mentally satisfied pet.

Interactive Play and Activities

Interactive play and activities are essential components of a German Shepherd's daily routine, providing both physical exercise and mental stimulation. These activities foster a strong bond between the dog and its owner, promote healthy behaviors, and prevent boredom and destructive tendencies. Engaging in various interactive play sessions and activities ensures a well-rounded and happy dog.

Playing fetch is one of the most popular and effective interactive activities for German Shepherds. This game provides a high-energy workout and allows the dog to channel its natural instincts to chase and retrieve. Using a ball, frisbee, or other fetching toys, owners can create dynamic and engaging play sessions that keep the dog physically active and mentally engaged. Fetch can be played in different environments, such as parks, backyards, or beaches, providing variety and excitement for the dog.

A German Shepherd enthusiastically playing fetch with a frisbee in a park.

Tug-of-war is another interactive game that German Shepherds enjoy. This game allows the dog to use its strength and engage in a friendly competition with its owner. Tug-of-war can help build the dog's muscles, improve its grip strength, and provide an outlet for its natural instincts to pull and shake. It is important to play tug-of-war with rules to ensure the game remains safe and controlled, such as teaching the dog to release the toy on command and ending the game if the dog becomes overly aggressive or excited.

Interactive toys that challenge the dog's problem-solving skills can also provide valuable mental and physical stimulation. Toys that require the dog to manipulate pieces, press buttons, or solve puzzles to release treats or rewards keep the dog engaged and mentally sharp. These toys can be used during playtime or as part of a training session, providing a fun and rewarding experience for the dog.

Agility training is an excellent way to combine physical exercise and mental stimulation in an interactive and structured manner. Agility courses involve navigating various obstacles, such as jumps, tunnels, and weave poles, which challenge the dog's physical abilities and cognitive skills. Participating in agility training helps build the dog's confidence, improves its coordination, and strengthens the bond between the dog and its owner through teamwork and communication.

A German Shepherd navigating an agility course, jumping over an obstacle.

Hide-and-seek is a fun and interactive game that German Shepherds enjoy. This game can be played indoors or outdoors and involves the owner hiding while the dog searches for them. Hide-and-seek taps into the dog's natural instincts to track and find, providing mental stimulation and strengthening the bond between the dog and its owner. Owners can make the game more challenging by hiding in different locations or using scent trails to guide the dog.

Interactive play sessions that involve teaching new tricks or commands can also be highly engaging for German Shepherds. These sessions provide mental stimulation and help reinforce positive behaviors. Teaching the dog to perform a series of tricks, such as spinning, rolling over, or playing dead, can be a fun and rewarding experience for both the dog and its owner. Using positive reinforcement techniques, such as treats, praise, and play, makes the training sessions enjoyable and effective.

Participating in dog sports, such as flyball, dock diving, or herding trials, can provide an excellent outlet for a German Shepherd's energy and natural abilities. These sports offer structured and competitive environments where the dog can engage in physical and mental challenges. Dog sports also provide opportunities for socialization with other dogs and handlers, contributing to the dog's overall well-being and social skills.

Incorporating interactive play and activities into a German Shepherd's daily routine is essential for its overall health and happiness. Games like fetch, tug-of-war, and hide-and-seek, along with agility training, interactive toys, trick training, and dog sports, provide a well-rounded and engaging experience for the dog. These activities help prevent boredom, reduce behavioral issues, and strengthen the bond between the dog and its owner, ensuring a happy, healthy, and well-adjusted pet.

CHAPTER 9
Health and Nutrition

Diet and Feeding Guidelines

Proper nutrition is fundamental to the health and well-being of any dog, particularly a high-energy breed like the German Shepherd. Understanding the dietary needs and feeding guidelines for this breed ensures optimal growth, development, and overall health.

German Shepherds require a balanced diet rich in high-quality protein, healthy fats, carbohydrates, vitamins, and minerals. Protein is crucial for muscle development and repair, especially in a breed known for its physical prowess and activity levels. Look for dog foods where the primary ingredient is a high-quality source of animal protein, such as chicken, beef, or fish. These proteins provide essential amino acids necessary for maintaining muscle mass and overall body function.

Fats are another vital component of a German Shepherd's diet. Healthy fats, such as those derived from fish oil, flaxseed, and chicken fat, supply essential fatty acids like Omega-3 and Omega-6. These fats support skin health, promote a shiny coat, aid in brain function, and provide a concentrated energy source.

While fats are necessary, they should be balanced with the overall caloric intake to prevent obesity.

Carbohydrates provide energy and support digestive health. Whole grains like brown rice, barley, and oats, as well as vegetables like sweet potatoes and peas, offer digestible sources of carbohydrates and fiber. Fiber is crucial for maintaining digestive health, helping to regulate the gastrointestinal tract and prevent issues such as constipation and diarrhea.

Vitamins and minerals are essential for various bodily functions, including immune system support, bone health, and metabolic processes. Commercial dog foods formulated for large breeds often contain a balanced mix of these nutrients. However, it's essential to choose a reputable brand that meets the standards set by the Association of American Feed Control Officials (AAFCO). These standards ensure that the food provides complete and balanced nutrition for the dog's specific life stage, whether they are puppies, adults, or seniors.

Puppies have different nutritional needs compared to adult and senior dogs. During the first year, German Shepherd puppies experience rapid growth, necessitating a diet that supports bone and muscle development. Puppy food should be rich in protein and calories, with the appropriate balance of calcium and phosphorus to support healthy skeletal growth. Overfeeding or providing an imbalanced diet during this critical period can lead to growth disorders and joint issues.

Adult German Shepherds require a maintenance diet that provides balanced nutrition to sustain their energy levels, muscle mass, and overall health. Portion control is crucial to prevent obesity, a common issue that can lead to various health problems, including joint stress and metabolic disorders. Regularly monitoring the dog's weight and adjusting portions as needed is essential.

Senior German Shepherds have different dietary requirements, often needing fewer calories due to a slower metabolism and reduced activity levels. Senior dog foods typically contain lower fat content and higher fiber to support digestive health. Additionally, these foods may include supplements like glucosamine and chondroitin to support joint health, which becomes increasingly important as dogs age.

A German Shepherd eating a balanced meal from a bowl.

Hydration is another critical aspect of a German Shepherd's diet. Fresh, clean water should always be available to prevent dehydration, support metabolic processes, and maintain overall health. Dehydration can lead to serious health issues, especially in active dogs that lose water through panting and exercise.

Feeding schedules should be consistent, with most adult German Shepherds benefiting from being fed twice a day—once in the morning and once in the evening. Puppies, on the other hand, may require more frequent feedings, typically three to four times a day, to support their rapid growth and high energy levels. Establishing a regular feeding routine helps regulate the dog's metabolism and can prevent issues such as bloat, which German Shepherds are prone to.

In addition to commercial dog food, some owners opt for home-cooked meals or raw diets, known as BARF (Biologically Appropriate Raw Food). While these diets can be beneficial, they require careful planning and a thorough understanding of canine nutrition to ensure they meet all the dog's dietary needs. Consulting with a veterinarian or a canine nutritionist is essential before starting a home-cooked or raw diet.

Treats are a valuable tool for training and rewarding good behavior but should be given in moderation. Treats should not exceed 10% of the dog's daily caloric intake to avoid unbalanced nutrition and weight gain. Opt for healthy treats, such as small pieces of cooked meat, vegetables, or commercial treats formulated for dogs.

A balanced diet tailored to the specific needs of a German Shepherd at different life stages is crucial for maintaining their health and vitality. Regularly consulting with a veterinarian to assess the dog's nutritional needs and adjust their diet as needed helps ensure they receive the best possible care.

Routine Veterinary Care

Routine veterinary care is essential for maintaining the health and well-being of a German Shepherd. Regular check-ups, vaccinations, parasite prevention, and dental care are all critical components of a comprehensive healthcare plan.

Annual veterinary check-ups are crucial for early detection and prevention of health issues. During these visits, the veterinarian will perform a thorough physical examination, checking the dog's weight, coat condition, teeth, eyes, ears, and overall body condition. Regular blood tests and urinalysis can help detect underlying health problems, such as kidney or liver disease, before they become severe.

Vaccinations are a vital part of preventive healthcare. German Shepherds should receive core vaccines, which protect against common and potentially deadly diseases such as rabies, distemper, parvovirus, and adenovirus. Depending on the dog's lifestyle and exposure risk, the veterinarian may recommend additional vaccines, such as those for bordetella (kennel cough), Lyme disease, and leptospirosis.

Parasite prevention is another critical aspect of routine veterinary care. German Shepherds should be protected against common parasites, including fleas, ticks, and heartworms. Monthly preventive treatments are available in various forms, such as topical applications, oral medications, and collars. Regular fecal examinations are also essential to check for intestinal parasites like roundworms, hookworms, and giardia, which can be transmitted to humans and other pets.

Dental care is often overlooked but is vital for a German Shepherd's overall health. Dental disease can lead to pain, tooth loss, and systemic health issues, including heart, liver, and kidney problems. Regular dental check-ups and cleanings by a veterinarian help prevent dental disease. At-home dental care, such as brushing the dog's teeth with canine toothpaste and providing dental chews, can also help maintain oral health.

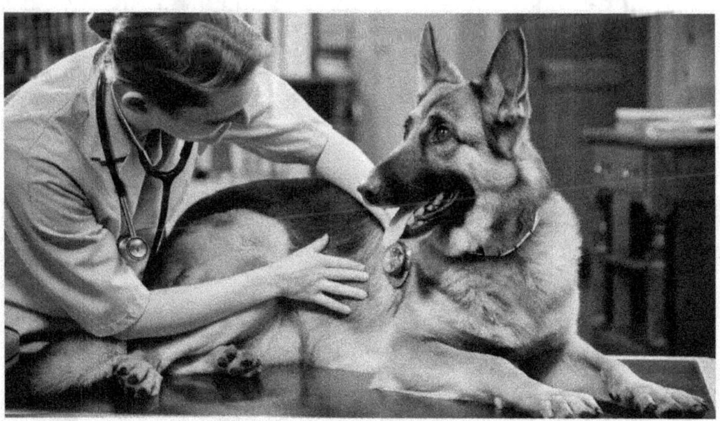

A veterinarian examining a German Shepherd during a routine check-up.

Spaying or neutering is recommended for most German Shepherds unless they are intended for breeding. This procedure not only helps control the pet population but also reduces the risk of certain health issues, such as mammary tumors, pyometra (a severe uterine infection), and testicular cancer. Spaying or neutering is typically performed when the dog is between six months to one year old, although the timing may vary based on the veterinarian's advice.

In addition to regular veterinary visits, it is essential to monitor a German Shepherd's health at home. This includes checking for signs of illness or discomfort, such as changes in appetite, water consumption, energy levels, behavior, and physical appearance. Early detection of health issues can lead to more effective treatment and better outcomes.

Maintaining a health record for the German Shepherd, including vaccination dates, medications, and any health issues or treatments, is crucial. This information can be invaluable for the veterinarian and helps ensure that the dog receives consistent and comprehensive care.

Routine veterinary care is vital for preventing and managing health issues in German Shepherds. Regular check-ups, vaccinations, parasite prevention, dental care, and monitoring at home all contribute to a comprehensive healthcare plan that supports the dog's overall health and well-being.

Recognizing Health Issues

Recognizing health issues early can significantly impact the treatment and management of various conditions in German Shepherds. Being aware of common health problems and their symptoms allows for prompt veterinary intervention and improves the dog's quality of life.

One of the most common health issues in German Shepherds is hip dysplasia, a genetic condition where the hip joint does not develop properly, leading to arthritis and pain. Early signs of hip dysplasia include limping, difficulty rising, reluctance to climb stairs or jump, and a decrease in activity levels. Regular veterinary check-ups and X-rays can help diagnose this condition early, and treatments such as weight management, joint supplements, physical therapy, and, in severe cases, surgery can help manage the symptoms.

Elbow dysplasia is another common joint issue in German Shepherds. Similar to hip dysplasia, it involves abnormal development of the elbow joint, leading to pain and arthritis. Symptoms include lameness in the front legs, swelling, and difficulty with mobility. Early diagnosis and management through weight control, physical therapy, and medication can help improve the dog's quality of life.

Degenerative myelopathy is a progressive spinal cord disease that affects German Shepherds. This condition leads to a gradual loss of coordination and mobility in the hind legs, eventually resulting in paralysis. Early signs include dragging the hind legs, difficulty standing, and wobbling. While there is no cure for degenerative myelopathy, physical therapy, supportive devices like harnesses, and a well-managed care plan can help slow the progression and maintain the dog's quality of life for as long as possible.

Bloat, or gastric dilatation-volvulus (GDV), is a life-threatening condition that affects large, deep-chested breeds like German Shepherds. Bloat occurs when the stomach fills with gas and twists, cutting off blood flow and leading to shock and tissue death. Symptoms include a swollen abdomen, restlessness, drooling, and attempts to vomit without producing anything. Bloat requires immediate veterinary intervention, often involving emergency surgery. Preventive measures include feeding smaller, more frequent meals, avoiding vigorous exercise immediately after eating, and using elevated feeding bowls.

Exocrine pancreatic insufficiency (EPI) is a condition where the pancreas does not produce enough digestive enzymes, leading to malabsorption and malnutrition. German Shepherds are predisposed to this condition, which manifests as chronic diarrhea, weight loss despite a good appetite, and a poor coat condition. EPI is diagnosed through blood tests and treated with enzyme replacement therapy, which typically involves adding pancreatic enzymes to the dog's food.

Allergies, both food-related and environmental, are also common in German Shepherds. Symptoms include itching, ear infections, gastrointestinal issues, and skin infections. Identifying and eliminating the allergen, whether it is a specific ingredient in the diet or an environmental factor like pollen, is crucial for managing allergies. Veterinary guidance and testing can help pinpoint the cause and develop an appropriate treatment plan, which may include dietary changes, medications, and lifestyle adjustments.

German Shepherds are also prone to heart conditions, such as dilated cardiomyopathy (DCM), where the heart becomes enlarged and weakened. Symptoms of heart disease include coughing, difficulty breathing, fatigue, and fainting. Regular veterinary check-ups, including cardiac exams and imaging, can help detect heart issues early. Treatment may involve medications to manage symptoms and improve heart function.

Thyroid disorders, particularly hypothyroidism, are common in German Shepherds. Hypothyroidism occurs when the thyroid gland does not produce enough thyroid hormone, leading to symptoms such as weight gain, lethargy, hair loss, and skin issues. Blood tests can diagnose hypothyroidism, and treatment typically involves daily thyroid hormone replacement medication.

Recognizing behavioral changes is also crucial in identifying health issues. Changes in behavior, such as increased aggression, anxiety, or lethargy, can indicate underlying health problems that require veterinary attention.

Being vigilant and proactive in recognizing health issues in German Shepherds ensures timely veterinary care and better management of conditions. Understanding common health problems and their symptoms, combined with regular veterinary check-ups and a comprehensive healthcare plan, helps maintain the dog's health and quality of life.

Diet and feeding guidelines, routine veterinary care, and the ability to recognize health issues are all essential aspects of ensuring the health and well-being of German Shepherds. Providing balanced nutrition, maintaining regular veterinary visits, and being attentive to signs of illness or discomfort contribute to a comprehensive approach to the care and management of this remarkable breed.

CHAPTER 10

Maintaining Training

Continuing Education for Your Dog

Continuing education for dogs is crucial in ensuring they remain well-behaved, mentally stimulated, and responsive to commands throughout their lives. Just as humans benefit from lifelong learning, dogs also need ongoing training and new challenges to keep their minds sharp and behaviors in check. This is particularly important for intelligent and active breeds like the German Shepherd.

Ongoing training sessions provide numerous benefits. First, they reinforce good behavior and ensure that previously learned commands remain fresh in the dog's mind. Dogs can easily forget commands if they are not regularly practiced, leading to decreased obedience and potential behavioral issues. Consistent training helps solidify these commands and improves the dog's overall responsiveness.

Continuing education also addresses behavioral changes that may arise as the dog ages. Puppies, adults, and senior dogs all have different needs and may develop new behavioral challenges as they progress through life stages. Ongoing training allows for the adaptation of techniques to meet these changing needs, ensuring the dog remains well-behaved and mentally engaged.

Training can be a fun and rewarding experience for both the dog and the owner. Introducing new commands, tricks, or activities can provide mental stimulation and prevent boredom. For example, agility training, scent work, or advanced obedience can challenge a dog's intellect and physical abilities. These activities also provide an excellent opportunity for bonding between the dog and its owner, strengthening their relationship.

A German Shepherd participating in an agility training session.

Refreshing and Reinforcing Commands

Refreshing and reinforcing commands is an integral part of continuing education for dogs. Even well-trained dogs can become rusty if their skills are not regularly practiced. Refreshing commands ensures that the dog remains responsive and obedient, reducing the risk of undesirable behaviors.

One effective way to refresh commands is through regular short training sessions. These sessions do not need to be lengthy; five to ten minutes of focused training a few times a week can be sufficient. During these sessions, revisit basic commands such as sit, stay, come, and down. Reinforce these commands with positive reinforcement techniques, such as treats, praise, and play, to keep the dog motivated and engaged.

Incorporating training into daily routines can also be beneficial. For example, practice the sit command before feeding the dog or the stay command when opening the door for visitors. This not only refreshes the commands but also helps integrate them into everyday life, making them more practical and useful.

Using a variety of rewards can keep training interesting for the dog. While treats are a common reward, toys, playtime, and verbal praise can also be effective. Varying the rewards helps maintain the dog's interest and enthusiasm for training sessions.

Addressing any regression or new behavioral issues promptly is important in reinforcing commands. If a dog starts ignoring commands or developing unwanted behaviors, it is essential to revisit and reinforce the basic training principles. Consistency is key; ensure that all family members are using the same commands and rewards to avoid confusing the dog.

Advanced training classes can provide additional opportunities to refresh and reinforce commands. These classes often introduce new challenges and distractions, helping to solidify the dog's obedience in different environments and situations. Working with a professional trainer can also provide valuable insights and techniques for addressing specific behavioral issues.

Adapting Training to Life Stages

Adapting training to a dog's life stages is crucial for maintaining its overall well-being and ensuring its training remains relevant and effective. Different life stages bring different physical, mental, and behavioral changes that require adjustments in training techniques and goals.

Puppyhood is a critical period for socialization and basic training. During this stage, puppies are highly impressionable and can quickly learn new commands and behaviors. Focus on socializing the puppy with different people, animals, and environments to build a well-rounded and confident dog. Basic commands such as sit, stay, come, and leave should be introduced early on, using positive reinforcement to create a positive association with training.

Housebreaking and crate training are also essential during puppyhood. Consistency and patience are key, as puppies have short attention spans and may require frequent potty breaks. Establishing a routine and rewarding the puppy for successful potty trips and calm behavior in the crate can help accelerate the housebreaking process.

As the dog enters adolescence, it may test boundaries and exhibit more independent or challenging behaviors. This stage requires reinforcing existing commands and addressing any emerging behavioral issues. Consistency and patience are crucial during this time, as adolescent dogs may go through phases of testing limits and pushing boundaries. Continuing socialization and introducing new commands or activities can help keep the dog engaged and prevent boredom.

Adulthood is typically a more stable period, but ongoing training and mental stimulation remain important. Advanced training classes, agility courses, or other dog sports can provide physical and mental challenges that keep the dog sharp and well-behaved. Regularly refreshing and reinforcing commands helps maintain the dog's obedience and responsiveness.

Senior dogs may experience physical and cognitive changes that require adaptations in training. While older dogs may not be as physically active, mental stimulation is still crucial. Training sessions should be shorter and less physically demanding, focusing on maintaining cognitive function and preventing boredom. Commands like stay, sit, and come should continue to be practiced, but consider adjusting the difficulty level to match the dog's capabilities.

Incorporating low-impact activities such as scent work or gentle obedience training can provide mental stimulation for senior dogs. These activities challenge the dog's mind without putting undue stress on its body. Additionally, maintaining a consistent routine and providing a comfortable and supportive environment can help senior dogs feel secure and content.

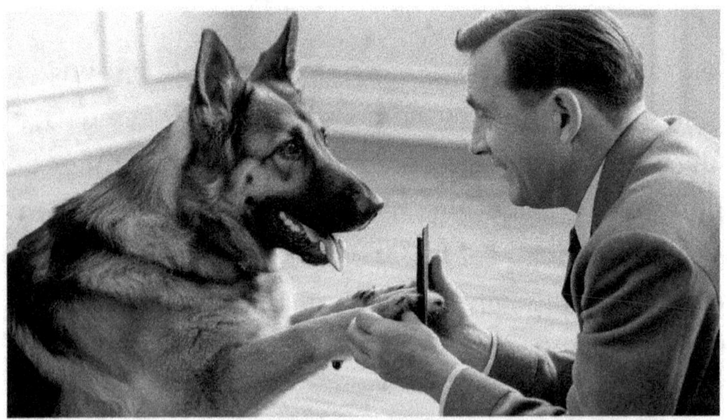

A senior German Shepherd participating in a gentle training session with its owner.

Training adaptations should also consider any health issues the dog may develop as it ages. Joint problems, vision or hearing loss, and other age-related conditions may impact the dog's ability to perform certain commands or activities. Consulting with a veterinarian and adjusting the training plan to accommodate these changes is essential for maintaining the dog's quality of life.

Continuing education for dogs through refreshing and reinforcing commands, as well as adapting training to different life stages, is vital for maintaining their obedience, mental stimulation, and overall well-being. Regular training sessions, consistency, and positive reinforcement help ensure that dogs remain responsive and well-behaved throughout their lives. Adapting training techniques and goals to match the dog's age and capabilities ensures that training remains effective and enjoyable for both the dog and its owner.

CHAPTER 11

CONCLUSION

Celebrating Progress and Success

Celebrating progress and success in dog training is essential for maintaining motivation and acknowledging the hard work put in by both the dog and the owner. Each milestone, no matter how small, deserves recognition. Celebrations can range from simple verbal praise and extra playtime to special treats or a favorite activity. Recognizing progress reinforces positive behavior and encourages continued effort.

Training a dog is a cumulative process, with each small achievement building towards larger goals. For example, a puppy learning to sit on command is the first step towards more complex behaviors like staying and coming when called. Celebrating these early successes lays a strong foundation for future training endeavors.

Acknowledging progress also helps in identifying areas that need further work. It provides an opportunity to reflect on what training methods are effective and which ones may need adjustment. This reflective practice ensures that the training approach remains dynamic and responsive to the dog's needs and learning style.

Public recognition can also be beneficial. Participating in dog training classes or groups where the dog's progress is acknowledged by trainers and peers can boost the dog's confidence and the owner's satisfaction. Competing in dog sports or obedience trials provides a formal setting to celebrate success and see the tangible results of training efforts.

A proud German Shepherd with its owner holding a ribbon from a dog training competition.

Building a Lifelong Bond

The process of training a German Shepherd extends far beyond teaching commands; it is about building a lifelong bond between the dog and the owner. This bond is rooted in trust, mutual respect, and understanding. Training sessions provide a unique opportunity to communicate and connect with the dog, establishing a relationship based on clear expectations and consistent reinforcement.

Trust is a fundamental element in this bond. A dog that trusts its owner is more likely to respond positively to training and exhibit good behavior. Trust is built through consistent, fair, and positive interactions. Using positive reinforcement techniques, such as rewarding good behavior with treats, praise, or play, helps foster this trust.

Mutual respect is equally important. Understanding the dog's needs, limitations, and capabilities shows respect for the animal's individuality. Training should always be conducted with patience and kindness, avoiding harsh punishments or negative reinforcement, which can damage the relationship and the dog's willingness to learn.

Communication is the cornerstone of a strong bond. Effective training requires clear and consistent commands, as well as attentive listening to the dog's signals and responses. Over time, this mutual communication enhances the understanding and cooperation between the dog and the owner, making training more effective and enjoyable.

Building a lifelong bond through training also involves spending quality time together outside of formal training sessions. Regular playtime, walks, and interactive activities strengthen the relationship and provide additional opportunities for bonding. These shared experiences contribute to a deeper connection and a happier, more well-adjusted dog.

Final Tips and Encouragement

Embarking on the journey of training a German Shepherd can be challenging, but it is important to stay motivated and positive. Here are some final tips and words of encouragement to support you through this rewarding experience:

Be Patient and Consistent: Training takes time, and progress can be slow. Patience and consistency are key. Stick to a regular training schedule, and consistently use the same commands and rewards. This helps the dog understand what is expected and builds reliable behaviors.

Stay Positive: Use positive reinforcement to encourage good behavior. Reward the dog immediately after it performs the desired action. This creates a positive association with the behavior and increases the likelihood of it being repeated.

Adapt to Your Dog's Needs: Every dog is unique, and what works for one may not work for another. Be flexible and willing to adapt your training methods to suit your dog's personality, age, and learning style. Pay attention to your dog's signals and adjust your approach as needed.

Keep Training Sessions Short and Fun: Dogs, especially young ones, have short attention spans. Keep training sessions brief, focused, and fun to maintain the dog's interest and enthusiasm. End each session on a positive note with a successful command or a fun activity.

Use a Variety of Rewards: Mixing up rewards can keep the dog motivated. While treats are effective, toys, praise, and playtime are also valuable rewards. Find what excites and motivates your dog the most and use it to reinforce good behavior.

Socialize Your Dog: Exposing your German Shepherd to different environments, people, and animals is crucial for developing a well-rounded and confident dog. Socialization helps prevent behavioral issues and ensures the dog is comfortable in various situations.

Seek Professional Help When Needed: If you encounter specific challenges or behavioral issues, do not hesitate to seek help from a professional dog trainer or behaviorist. They can provide tailored advice and support to address your dog's needs.

Celebrate Small Victories: Every step forward, no matter how small, is worth celebrating. Recognizing and rewarding progress keeps the training process positive and encourages continued effort.

Training a German Shepherd is a journey that requires dedication, but the rewards are immense. The bond formed through consistent training, the joy of celebrating progress, and the satisfaction of having a well-behaved companion are invaluable. Remember, training is not just about obedience; it is about building a deep, trusting relationship that lasts a lifetime.

Creating a training schedule for your German Shepherd ensures consistency and helps you cover all aspects of their development. Below are three templates to guide

you through different stages: Puppy Training, Adolescent
Training, and Adult Training.

www.ingramcontent.com/pod-product-compliance
Lightning Source LLC
Chambersburg PA
CBHW051603250726

48653CB00004BA/1310